MORE PRAISE FOR

"A much-needed cleansing agent for the dogmatic certainty that infects so much of today's public discourse."

— Don Lattin, *San Francisco Chronicle*

"In his role on *Forum*, Krasny is known for being a thoughtful, even-handed moderator who respects diverse opinions. He sought to bring a similar mind-set to *Spiritual Envy....* Krasny breaks down the fundamental differences between agnostics and atheists, examines the prohibitions set forth in the Ten Commandments, and presents a passionate case for religious tolerance."

— *Mercury News*

"According to the public-opinion polls, agnostics and atheists are the group Americans trust least — even though nonbelievers conduct themselves *more* ethically than do the religious faithful. It helps in reducing such ignorance and fear for nonbelievers to come out of the closet and profess not only their opinions but the emotional and intellectual struggles behind them, as the always engaging Michael Krasny does in this probing examination of his spirituality and ours."

— Timothy Ferris, author of
Coming of Age in the Milky Way

"Michael Krasny's *Spiritual Envy* is a memoir of seeking and questioning, of a battle between a man's deepest yearnings and formidable intellect, of the longing for belief in the face of the impossibility of belief. If doubt is an element of faith, then Krasny's grappling with doubt is a kind of act of faith itself. This is a beautifully written book, and reading it is a spiritual adventure."

— Dani Shapiro, author of *Family History*

"An eloquent and deeply personal journey to find some kind of spiritual center in what has become an increasingly polarized debate about the role and function of religion in America."

— Reza Aslan, *The Daily Beast*

"The vitality and integrity of this beautifully written book is bound to touch anyone who knows how to value a truly independent mind and spirit."

— Jacob Needleman, author of *What Is God?*

"In this engrossing memoir, Michael Krasny searches for God and fails to find Him. Yet God finds Michael Krasny in the 'negative way' known so well to so many who seek Him. God is not an entity to be accessed and understood. God is love, infinite and eternal. To seek Him is to find Him, even as we envy those who have stumbled upon what they believe to be the answer."

— Kevin Starr, professor of history, University of Southern California

SPIRITUAL
ENVY

MICHAEL KRASNY

SPIRITUAL ENVY

AN AGNOSTIC'S QUEST

Foreword by Joyce Carol Oates

New World Library
Novato, California

New World Library
14 Pamaron Way
Novato, California 94949

Text design by Tona Pearce Myers

Library of Congress Cataloging-in-Publication Data
Krasny, Michael, date.
Spiritual envy : an agnostic's quest / Michael Krasny ; foreword by
  Joyce Carol Oates.
    p. cm.
Includes index.
ISBN 978-1-57731-912-2 (hardcover : alk. paper)
  1. Agnosticism. 2. Krasny, Michael, date.—Religion. I. Title.
BL2747.2.K73 2010
211'.7—dc22   2010029392

First paperback printing, January 2012
ISBN 978-1-60868-069-6
Printed in the USA on 100% postconsumer-waste recycled paper

New World Library is a proud member of the Green Press Initiative.

10 9 8 7 6 5 4 3 2 1

To my father and mother,
Hyman "Zaz" Krasny and Betty Krasny.
If memory is blessed, you both are there.

The important thing is not to stop questioning.

—— ALBERT EINSTEIN

Contents

Foreword

Spiritual Envy: An Agnostic's Quest is both a strikingly original, boldly candid, and poignant memoir of one man's dramatic experience with "faith" and a kind of everyman's pilgrimage with special resonance for contemporary Americans who came of age in the 1950s and 1960s. The author's voice is wonderfully frank, conversational, and illuminating — Michael Krasny seems to have read virtually everything relevant to his thorny topic and has fresh and original things to say about what he has read. This "agnostic's quest" might also be called an "agnostic's handbook" — nothing could be more timely!

— Joyce Carol Oates

Introduction

After I published my memoir, *Off Mike: A Memoir of Talk Radio and Literary Life*, I began to think a lot about goodness. I had written about wanting, as a young man, to find an answer to the question of how a good man should live, which had first struck me with considerable impact when I read the work of Nobel Prize–winning novelist Saul Bellow. But the question that intrigued me even more, I realized after my book came out, was: why choose to be good?

Why strive for goodness? The answer for many nonbelievers is either humanism or a secular code of their own, but for most the answer has traditionally led to or been based on faith. I began to wonder if I could or should write about faith even though my adult life has been more about seeking than finding. Sam Harris had published *The End of Faith*, in which he made a number of estimable points in his screed against faith. But I recalled a conversation I had had with Daniel Goleman, the author of *Emotional Intelligence*, in which he told me, "I know Sam. He's an ideologue." "Yes!" I thought, "and so are most of the new wave of atheists who offer screeds against faith and excoriate religion and its bloody history and the cruel and despicable deeds done in its name." Harris said, "Science must destroy religion"; atheist Richard Dawkins compared religious education to child abuse; while Christopher Hitchens, the author of *God Is Not Great*, spoke of the need to prepare for a war against religion.

I could not call myself a man of faith, but if ideology-smitten atheists could write of faith, why not a skeptic who envied those who, without being coercive or intolerant, were fortunate enough to have it? I had not made the leap to faith since losing it somewhere between adolescence and young adulthood. Moreover, I was bereft of answers. I had been, for most of my adult life, in a state of uncertainty about age-old metaphysical questions concerning God's existence, good and evil, spirituality, and the meaning of life, questions that matter greatly to thinking people. But I also wasn't willing to call myself a nonbeliever, because I wasn't certain about the accuracy of characterizing what I had as the absence of belief. I was, I realized, a doubter, an agnostic, and, like perhaps hundreds of thousands of others, a seeker.

Mostly I have sought knowledge, with the hope that knowledge would lead to the kind of faith that would undergird my existence. I longed to find answers, to pierce, even momentarily, the veil that prevents us from understanding the essential questions of our existence. Is there a higher power? If so, what is its nature or way of manifesting? Was Moses given commandments on Sinai? Should we obey those commandments even if we cannot know or be certain of God or of his having handed them down? If we cannot know or be certain of God, can we determine, without God, what is moral or good? Where or how do we find meaning?

Who was I to take on such monumental and elemental questions? It was true that I had spent my adult life seeking answers to these questions and leading conversations on nearly every imaginable topic with some of the world's greatest writers and thinkers, both as a university professor and as host of a popular public radio program. But to try to bring light to timeless and essential questions about our existence seemed at best a foolish endeavor and at worst an exercise in hubris and futility. Yet some indeterminate force was driving me to write about these matters, and I realized that if there was indeed an article of faith I believed in, it was the notion that writing brings insight and ultimately, even profoundly, affects thought and discourse. How do we know, when we write or paint or sculpt or talk on the radio or do good works, that we are not tapping into a mystery beyond our unconscious? Is there a way to determine what a higher purpose is or can be?

I was struck by a memorable line from the British writer Julian Barnes, who said, "I don't believe in God but I miss him." That statement resonated for me, not so much the part about not believing, but the part about missing. As a boy I was certain God was with me, watching over me, a friend and confidant I could rely on. I knew he was there for me, wherever "there" happened to be. I believed in God even when I got the worst beating of my life from my sixth grade teacher, a cockney Brit who would erupt in rage and haul me into the boy's bathroom for a flurry of slaps and punches and kicks, and who, on one occasion, thrust my eleven-year-old head into the toilet for a cruel dunk. Because I was a kid who misbehaved, I felt the physical abuse I received was justified and my bad behavior its cause. Which is why I never told anyone, including my parents. But I was intelligent enough to dedicate myself to reforming my behavior so I wouldn't continue to be taken to the boys' restroom. I let it be known that I was the new Michael Krasny, a Michael Krasny who had metamorphosed into a good boy.

I became my teacher's helpmate, staying late after school and assisting him with cleaning the room, putting up and taking down class drawings, and doing anything else he bid me to do. I did these good-boy deeds cheerfully and dependably because I wanted his goodwill and approval. I was determined to make him know I could be good, and thus stave off his violence and see it replaced by a teacher's affection. It worked until one day after school when I was carrying a bucket of paint for him to another sixth grade classroom. I slipped and helplessly watched as the bucket toppled over and yellow paint flowed down the elementary school corridor like a miniature river. My teacher saw it all while hastening out of the classroom for a cigarette, and he erupted into a rage that led to the most ferocious of all the assaults. I got a beating in the boys' room, followed by his ordering me to mop up the paint, which I did, suffering in silence, holding in my tears until I had finished and left the school grounds. Lest somebody see me cry, I waited until I got to a small wooded area near my home, where I was certain I could not be seen, and then sobbed convulsively, saying to myself, "I was being good. No one knows. But you do, God. You know."

. This sad tale from childhood seems almost like a parable now. I was good, and being good was not supposed to bring punishment. God knew I did not deserve that beating. God knew I had slipped. God knew everything, and heard me when I told him I knew he knew. Even an unjust and cruel beating could not diminish my belief in him or his omniscience. I use this episode to highlight a child's faith that, even in the wake of trauma, was impossible to diminish. It wasn't until years later, when doubt began to seep in, that I asked the often-asked but never-answered question of how a just God could allow a defenseless child to be beaten. But the larger and more poignant question turns out to be this: how can I or anyone else make up for the loss of a God who once felt real, comforting, close, and personal. How does one fill that vacuum?

The idea of a child being beaten or otherwise abused is frequently a litmus test for belief in God. How can the anthropomorphic God most mortals have believed in since polytheism first waned, the God who gave the commandments to Moses, allow violence against an innocent child? When I was a boy, the question never occurred to me. Years later, after I'd begun to think seriously about faith, I came to recognize that having faith might mean being blind, but it also meant being consoled in grief and not needing answers. To the agnostic, such faith is nothing but the wind whispering, the clouds vanishing. To the agnostic, faith cannot come except in response to some form of proof. What is one to do with the recognition of complete uncertainty, the recognition that matters beyond the physical world are more mysterious even than our observable world and its host of impenetrable mysteries — the migrations of birds and butterflies, the mating of emperor penguins, unrequited love, the evil that men and women do?

When I write of spiritual envy, I mean envy of the consolation of faith, of the elevating power of knowing a force or forces beyond the physical, observable world or past the finite limits of self, of knowing a higher purpose, or possessing answers, or even being convinced they can be discovered. To have answers and certainty, to possess spiritual anchoring or spiritual authority and purpose, is to have comfort, a release from the entrapment of life's suffering. And even though religion has been much maligned in recent years — and deservedly so for having led too many in its name along dark paths of cruelty, intransigence, self-righteousness, and violence — religion also has provided ineffable solace and a reason for living a moral life, a reason for charity and generosity.

I knew I did not have answers or certainty or even knowledge of the route to travel for a spiritual quest. But my uncertainty and lack of answers were what I needed in order to engage. I could not embrace belief or find answers that put my restless mind to rest. But as I have discovered in pursuing knowledge, illumination can emerge from writing and from asking the right questions, even if answers are not to be found.

Asking the right questions is at the heart of agnosticism, for it is essentially about uncertainty. The word *agnosticism* has become identified with nearly all forms of uncertainty and indecision, and with simply the position of waiting for the correct, or at least a satisfactory, answer. Agnosticism is a position that denies the existence of absolutes and hidden spiritual forces behind the natural or material world until they can be empirically proven. Agnosticism welcomes proof, craves it, demands it. It does not say there is no God. It also does not say there is one. God's existence, in whatever form, cannot be proven, but neither can God's nonexistence. Agnosticism stands open to verification of either side of the God question and of every other major metaphysical question devoid of demonstrable proof. Though most agnostics eschew organized religion, many, even in their cloud of uncertainty, often take comfort in religious ritual, practice, ceremony, and community. Thus agnosticism differs markedly from atheism, which represents a categorical denial of God's existence and more often a flat rejection of any and all religious ritual, practice, ceremony, and community. Agnosticism does not preclude spiritual hunger. Agnostics possessed of spiritual hunger can and do envy those with spiritual sustenance.

The inescapable paradox for agnostics is that, with increased knowledge, especially in the past hundred years or so, we have seen corresponding greater ignorance and uncertainty. Only a century ago the Milky Way was thought to be the entire cosmos, and now we know there are a hundred billion observable galaxies. The more we have learned about the universe, the more mysterious it has proven to be, and we now have the respected hypothesis that there are perhaps many universes. Quantum physics gives us the multiverse hypothesis, which, like God, is plausible but presently beyond proof.

As we have applied historical and archaeological scholarship to our understanding of the scriptures and holy books, it has undermined faith and created greater uncertainty about what has long been regarded as the word of God. This has not been the case among what I call the true believers, however, those irretrievably tied to fundamentalist Christianity, Orthodox Judaism, or religious Islam. Most true believers, it would seem, have remained immovable in their faith even as knowledge has advanced and made uncertainty appear more certain and literal interpretations of holy texts impossible to accept without the bulwark of strong and unbending faith. Religious dogmatism has paradoxically helped to ignite greater and wider secularism, as well as prompted new clerical explanations and interpretations anchored in metaphor and myth. But this dogmatism has also hardened into a more unrelenting insistence on the word of God even in the wake of all the uncertainty and despite the alleged word of God being available only in translation.

This is a book for seekers who long for answers. Answers,

however, lead to some of the most vexing philosophical questions of our civilization's history, and so the book is designed as an investigation into the nature of spiritual-truth-seeking and as an aid in the quest for a moral code. It is also a book about agnosticism. Much polemical writing on atheism, and on perceived religious or spiritual truth, exists in the world; but, I discovered, there is little of especially recent vintage that offers a deep or truly meaningful exploration of agnosticism. The relevance and legitimacy of agnostic thinking was important for me to explore and write about. As I plunged deeper into the subject, I realized I also wanted to consider some of the major agnostic thinkers, such as Darwin's bulldog, Thomas H. Huxley, who gave us the word *agnostic*, and Robert Ingersoll, who was known as "the great agnostic," as well as the celebrated philosopher Bertrand Russell, who was inclined to call himself both an atheist and an agnostic.

The agnostic waits to find spiritual truth and often, in waiting, envies those who no longer wait or who maintain certainty. This includes those who refuse to subscribe to any individual religion or belief but feel certain they have discovered a higher or ennobling spiritual truth or an entrance to it. This, then, is a book about waiting and seeking, about agnosticism, good and evil, spiritual envy, and what may quite possibly be life's most important questions.

Chapter 1

MY GOD

As a boy I used to imagine that God was watching over me and could do anything he wanted with me, could move the chess pieces of my life to any spot on the board he chose, but would not, as Shakespeare would have it in *King Lear*, play with me as a wanton boy plays with flies. I trusted him. How could I not? God suffused my young life. I felt he (I use the male pronoun for convenience and because he was solely a he to me) was a companion, a presence with whom I could share my most secret thoughts and fears and wants.

My parents were believers, and while my doubts spread as I grew into young manhood, my mother was certain that God marked down even our smallest lies and indiscretions. She would speak of God as the creator who had filled the world with an amazing range and variety of people, and she spoke with near wonder at how the differences in people were what God handed out at birth — talents and abilities, defects and disabilities, handsomeness and ugliness. To her, the beauty of the divinity was in the wondrous diversity and breadth of human creations, the miraculous feats of a master builder. "God made no two people the same. Not even twins," she would say. "And," she assured me, "God gave you many blessings he did not give to others."

My supposed good looks and intelligence and winning personality, which a loving Jewish mother complimented and brightened at, were gifts handed to me at birth by God himself. Such notions sustained me like mother's milk. They were difficult to shake even as I was increasingly drawn away from belief. When as a young child I asked my mother how I was born and came to be, she had a stock answer: "Your father planted the seeds, and we prayed to God." So I imagined my parents getting a package of seeds like the ones on the rack of flower and vegetable seeds sold at the pharmacy in our Cleveland Heights neighborhood. And for many years the facts of life to me meant planting seeds, as one did in order to grow roses or asparagus, but with a requisite preconception prayer to God. In my mind, childbirth depended on God's allowing planted seeds to grow. My entering the world was the result of God answering my parents' prayers.

As a boy I liked feeling God was my father. I loved my biological father and tried to honor him as the commandment dictated. But he worked terribly long hours and came home too tired to do anything but eat supper, read the newspaper, and head off to sleep. If he told me he loved me, he did so only on rare occasions, usually when I was being disciplined or if I became ill. He would say, "You know your father loves you." It was never "I love you." It was always "Your father loves you." I desperately wanted his attention. I wanted above all in life to know he cared about me and loved me. It was the same with God. I wanted to know he approved of me. I wanted to make both him and my earthly father proud. How could I be certain of God's love or my father's? How much did my heavenly and earthly fathers even like me?

I had an imaginary friend who had a full name — Michael Berber. I also had Sammy Kaye. Doubtless out of father hunger, I announced one day that Sammy Kaye, the bandleader, was my second father. God was my imaginary friend, too, but he was also, like Sammy Kaye, my imaginary father. Was he imaginary? He surely seemed real to me then, even if I vested him with a reality formed from my imagination, a reality that many who exalt art tell us is superior to the reality we identify as *the* reality. As a kid I watched *Miracle on 34th Street*, with Maureen O'Hara and Natalie Wood, the warm and bathetic Christmas story of Kris Kringle, played by Edmund Gwenn, who claimed he was the real Santa Claus. When the child played by Natalie Wood sat on his lap and asked him about the reality of Santa Claus, he told her there was another nation called the imagination, a line I fancied just as I fancied the sound of the word *Godspeed*, which concluded many orations. Was hunger for God simply a result of an oedipal need for a strong father who could be relied on for whatever one needed or longed for? Was the God whom I felt was my heavenly father merely a production of my seeded imagination? Was there such a thing as Godspeed?

When I write that God suffused my young boyhood, I mean it. The words *under God* were officially added to the Pledge of Allegiance when I was a boy, despite the many people who insisted on keeping them out. In courtroom television dramas like *Perry Mason*, men and women testified in court after putting a hand on the Bible and swearing to tell the whole truth and nothing but the truth so help them God. As youngsters we argued about God questions with a seriousness that bordered on passion. We did not argue about whether God existed, because for nearly all of us his existence was a given. What did it mean to take the Lord's name in vain? Were you even supposed to swear to God? (I remember a guy we called Tommy T saying, "I swear to God, I don't believe in God.") Could you say "goddamn"? Would God punish us for hanging out in the backyard of our neighbors' home at night to sneak peeks at their teenage daughter, Gloria, as she came into her bedroom naked after a bath? Would he exact payback for our chewing gum on Yom Kippur?

Kate Smith sang "God Bless America" on Ed Sullivan, and we all sang "America the Beautiful" in classrooms, asking God to shed his grace. The presidents ended their talks with "God bless America." Money said "In God we trust." Men and women who helped the poor and those who donated their time to charitable causes, as my mother did, were said to be doing God's work, and when the snow in Cleveland reached five or six inches we stayed home from school because of what was called an act of God. Something that occurred in the nick of time, a stroke of good fortune, was a Godsend, and one eluded an unhappy fate by the grace of God. God was the ultimate signifier. Adonai and Elohim and Ha Shem and Jehovah and all the various other names attributed to the invisible prime mover, the patriarch in the sky, were represented by that three-letter word. He was our God and the God of our fathers.

And he was my God. God Almighty. God the omnipotent. God the eternal, and God the everlasting. Nearly every Jewish home had a mezuzah outside its door with the Shema inscribed inside, words I said over and over and over again throughout my boyhood: "Hear oh Israel, the Lord our God. The Lord is one." It was God, after all, who had brought my people out of bondage and provided the perennial land grant that legitimated Israel as the promised land, the newly created state surrounded by bitter enemies. God was the father of us all. I knew by heart the Christian prayer that began: "Our father who art in heaven." He was our father and father to us all. He was my father, the force behind my existence and all others.

Before I learned to sing Christmas carols in school, I would get up on Sunday mornings, turn on the television, and watch programs about Jesus. There wasn't much else to watch on Sunday mornings in that era. I was just past kindergarten, and I recall asking my mother and her older sister, Pearl, when Jesus was going to return. They both seemed upset, though slightly bemused, that I had come to Jesus just by watching Sunday morning Christian television programming. I was put through a quick deprogramming of warnings about why as Jews we did not and could not accept Jesus as our savior. We were believers in one God, the only God, and Jesus was not his son. I was told that I, like all boys, was a son of God, but there was no single son of God who rose from the dead after being crucified. I was dismayed by my Aunt Pearl, who said to me, "Those Jesus stories you're watching are no more real than the cartoons." How could that be, I wondered? How could the television not be telling me the truth?

I remember the rejoicing when Israel became a state. A homeland for Jews at last after the Shoah, the massacres, the exterminations, the genocide. A homeland promised to the Jewish people by God himself, the God of Moses, the God who gave us the Torah and the Ten Commandments, the God of "America the Beautiful" and of the Pledge of Allegiance. The God in the Thanksgiving song I sang with a group of children onstage, and even the God whose alleged son I would sing Christmas carols to while knowing he was not

part of my religion. I could sing praises to Jesus without believing in him and without feeling any need for dreidel songs
or Jewish rock-of-ages songs to level the song-playing-field.
It didn't matter that I didn't believe in Jesus or his virgin birth.
I knew my God, and knew he was the real king of the Jews
and Israel, the land he made into a state. It was also the desert land the Jews made bloom. My mother led paper and or-
ange sales to benefit this land, we paid for trees that would be
planted in it, and we brought money for it to Hebrew school,
which we put in a little blue tin box. The land promised to my
ancestors.

I began to doubt God in high school. This is a common
enough story. I was immersing myself in books, trying to
make myself into an intellectual, discovering the worlds of
science and skepticism and free-range secular thinking. I read
Bertrand Russell and Charles Darwin, and I formed doubts
and the doubts worried me. I suddenly couldn't be absolutely
certain God did exist or that he was involved in my life.

When time passed and I became more informed, I wondered whether Arthur Koestler was possibly right that Russian
Jews like me and my family were descended from the Khazars, a band of quasi nomads of Turkic origin who converted
to Judaism, rather than from the ancient Hebrews. And what
was a Jewish agnostic — if that was what I was morphing into
— to do about Israel? Was belief in Israel, like the Ten Commandments, contingent on belief in God? If it was the promised land that God vowed to give his chosen people, then of
course it was our land and not the land of the Arabs who had
been living on it and growing olive trees in its soil, and who
were claiming it. Israel was the birthright of the Jewish people, and to many it was the sense that could be made out of the
sacrifice of millions who died from the flames and bullets and

poisons of the holocaust. Israel seemed to have more power over many of the Jews I knew and came in contact with than the Ten Commandments or any tenet of Judaism.

It seemed no accident that many Jews became ardent Zionists, socialists, communists, or feminists, as if they needed a surrogate, secular messianism to replace a more ineffable faith. People of all faiths and creeds began to have doubts. As my skepticism grew, I found that I wanted to hold on to my faith but still drew closer to agnosticism, even though *agnostic*, like *atheist*, felt like a word I could not attach myself to for fear that God, if he did exist, would punish me. Doubt did not have to mean abrogating God, did it? If God existed, how disloyal it would be to call myself an agnostic — even if I said it only to myself. My God knew my every thought and would be angry. If he did exist and loved me, I would be torn from his good graces.

As a boy I had been pious, more religious than my parents had ever dreamed I would be. With a skullcap on my head and cantorial training from the cantor's youth club, I led services and chanted Hebrew prayers like a kid smitten, which I was, with Elvis — in the pulpit I tried to sound like a rock-and-roll cantor. Before doubt began invading me, I tended an abiding faith in God and prayed to him nightly in intimate conversational and cathartic fashion. I was certain he was listening as I released my secret thoughts and wants, not necessarily expecting him to grant what I wanted or longed for, but knowing he heard me and took full account of all my thoughts and actions. Then I read an article in the *Reader's Digest*, one of the few written materials available in our house, aside from the Bible and the *Merck Manual*, kept on hand by my father, who was frustrated at not having become a doctor. The *Digest* article assured me that one should never pray for selfish wants or expect to be catered to by God. After reading the article, I feared asking God for much for myself, lest he think a vain wish should trump any deep fear I had about my safekeeping and the health and lives of my parents.

This went on for years, until I began to agonize over feelings of unrequited love in junior high school and broke my own rules by asking God, in my nightly prayers, for the girl I longed for, even though I assured him it was a prayer of lower importance. Safekeeping and protection were what mattered most. Wishes were, for the most part, to be reserved in case of emergencies; requests could be made only with utter discretion. I could, after all, wind up on crutches or in a wheelchair like kids who had polio — which, in the prevaccine era, I felt fortunate not to have. Polio could get me, as it had former president Franklin Delano Roosevelt and the children whose pictures I'd seen on the March of Dimes solicitations. It was, I believed, swimming around in ready-to-attack microbial formations in Cumberland, our local municipal swimming pool.

I was also afraid of wanton violence. I knew at too young an age that it was out there lurking like a hungry tiger. I knew my people had been indiscriminately slaughtered in ovens and by Zyklon B and firing squads. If I proved myself good enough, worthy enough, surely God would protect me and those I loved from disease, suffering, violence, and death.

To a boy who embraced the tenets of his faith, the Ten Commandments were to be obeyed without question. Obedience to God meant in return, I hoped, protection from harm. The Ten Commandments were not only the foundation of Mosaic Law but also the essence of what God wanted and demanded, and one could hitch one's faith to them. It seemed a pretty sweet deal if all I needed to do to please God and avoid his punishment was simply to obey those ten perfectly reasonable and easy-to-follow commandments. They could be carved in my heart for life as they had been carved by God himself on the stone tablets he handed down to Moses.

The Ten Commandments are the cornerstone of, and the linchpin between, two of the world's major religions. Both Christians and Jews perceive the sanctity and importance of the Ten Commandments, which, according to scripture, were given to Moses on Mount Sinai. But as doubt began to erode my certainty about God's existence and his role as stage manager of my life, I began to doubt the Ten Commandments too, because, like God and country, God and the commandments were inextricably linked. To doubt God was bad enough, but to doubt the laws God commanded us to follow was perhaps most dire. How could one doubt commandments such as those that forbade us to steal or kill, commandments that had become essential to Western law and fundamental to ethical precepts? Yet could one *not* doubt the law if one doubted the lawgiver? Despite absorbing, by high school, a lot of ideas from freethinkers, and despite undergoing a serious diminution of faith, I wasn't ready to break fully from what I had taken in from my mother, my father, and my religion.

Before doubt set in, I imagined my life as a kind of unfolding drama or opera or what today might pass for reality TV. And who was my audience? Why, God! God was watching over me and watching how I reacted to every incident, person, and event, large or small. And of course, he was judging me, keeping, like Santa in the Christmas song, tallies of the bad and good things I did ("so be good for goodness sake!"). I would sometimes imagine him experimenting with me, providing stimuli as a laboratory scientist does with a small mammal. I thought these thoughts and felt twinges of emotion as I moved beyond adolescence and into young manhood with the sense that God could not possibly be like I had imagined him as a boy.

Reason accounted for doubt. I reasoned that no one could know there was absolutely and incontrovertibly a God, but also that it was impossible to conclude there was not. People got ill, suffered, lost loved ones, and died without heavenly oversight or intervention, but did that mean there was no God? If he was overseeing the human domain, he had a lot to monitor. Was he, for example, watching over all those billions of Chinese commies and godless Russians? What if we tossed in the animal kingdom, down to the level of the phyla I had memorized for high school biology tests — Protozoa, Porifera, and Coelenterata? Or how about ants, spiders, and rodents? His power to be involved in the lives of all creatures seemed impossible. Yet how could we mere mortals hope to divine the divine or, if there was a divine, begin to comprehend it?

As the years went by, it was easier for me to dismiss the idea of God's direct involvement in human affairs. But it was not so easy to dismiss God from involvement in my life, or to dismiss the possibility of a mystery beyond human reckoning, or to cast off fears and superstitions that crept up alongside my uncertainty, such as my fear of the potential price of denying my God. Whenever my mother accidentally spilled salt, she would toss a few grains of it over her left shoulder. It seemed like superstitious nonsense to me, but I did it too, just as I picked up her habit of at times speaking the word *kinahora*, a Yiddish term meant to keep the evil eye or bad luck away, just as knocking on wood or spitting is meant to ward off the evil eye. I wondered whether deference to God worked in a similar way for those who had begun to feel unconvinced that the deity existed or to doubt his omnipotence.

Back when I was barely pubescent, I had begun to wonder about the roles that uncertainty, ritual conditioning, and superstition play in belief. What of my feelings of helplessness that made me long for a supreme being, and my need to believe in divine will, a power that would be there for me — wherever *there* was — and for those I loved? How much of God, my God, was really about me and my childhood needs? And what about the Ten Commandments, on which my faith and morality rested?

If God had some calculus, I reasoned in high school, by which he determined rewards and punishments, it was clearly beyond me. Too many God-deniers had not experienced punishment, and too many lovers of God had suffered, for me to sort it out. As Dostoyevsky said in *The Brothers Karamazov*, in a world without God anything was permissible. Children were beaten to death or starved or raped, or they suffered and died from incurable diseases. Job had suffered. Why? Was it simply to valorize faith, as Abraham was prepared to do when he was on the brink of sacrificing his firstborn? Richard Rubenstein asked in *After Auschwitz*: where was the God of our Jewish fathers and mothers when Jewish infants in the camps were shoveled into ovens, and Jews, gypsies, dissidents, and homosexuals were slaughtered like rats and chickens? If God cared a fig about the human species, why did he allow the staggering carnage of the death camps? These were the kinds of impossible questions that I, like many others at the time, was grappling with. By college, however, such questions seemed to boil down to my attempts to understand how a God who had handed down moral law on Sinai could allow pointless suffering rather than intervene in our lives. Perhaps if there was a God, God's ways were simply unknowable. Or perhaps there was no God!

I recall that, when I was a college senior, *Time* magazine
heralded, à la Nietzsche, the death of God. Denying God's
existence outright led me to Aristotle and to the Christian
theologian Paul Tillich, both of whom argued the idea of
negative affirmation. That is, if you say God does not exist,
you are really saying he does, because you can only deny that
which exists. By denying, you affirm. Curious reasoning. I remember thinking, if I said Neptune beings did not exist, did
that affirm life on Neptune? If I proclaimed the death of God,
was I affirming that he once lived, or that he presently was
alive; or was it all merely metaphor? To proclaim or accept
the death of a presence I had personally felt deeply bound to
seemed reckless. If God existed, how could I presume to kill
him or claim him dead or nonexistent? How could I simply
lose or abandon a presence that had earlier filled my life?

But here was the real rub. How could Nietzsche or *Time*
or anyone proclaim God dead if God's existence was unverifiable? Of course, the death of God was metaphoric. Nietzsche
wanted us to become, in the wake of his proclamation, super-
men who were not even vulnerable — like the comic book
character — to kryptonite. But the notion of God's being or
God's presumptive presence remained as far beyond me as
the distant stars. If there was a big bang, what was prior to it?
What conceived it? What presences were within the absences
beyond our senses or consciousness? All such questions, I realized early on, were unanswerable unless you believed you
had discovered truth or made the leap to faith.

Chapter 2

THE TEN COMMANDMENTS
AND GOD'S EXISTENCE

THE TEN COMMANDMENTS

1. Thou shalt have no other God before thy God.
2. Thou shalt have no graven images from heaven above or earth below or water under the earth.
3. Thou shalt not take the name of thy Lord God in vain.
4. Thou shalt remember the Sabbath Day and keep it holy.
5. Honor thy father and mother.
6. Thou shalt not kill.
7. Thou shalt not commit adultery.
8. Thou shalt not steal.
9. Thou shalt not bear false witness against thy neighbor.
10. Thou shalt not covet thy neighbor's house nor wife nor male servant nor female servant nor his ox, donkey, nor anything that is thy neighbor's.

To what extent, I began to wonder in my college years, was God's existence at stake when one reckoned with the Ten Commandments? Even secular humanists and nonbelievers vouched that the commandments were the foundation of Western civilization and, as such, deserved our compliance even if there was no God poised to reward or punish us. The commandments were sensible rules, even nonbelievers reasoned, by which to live one's life. They protected us from ourselves and others and ensured order over chaos, law over anarchy.

Tales in all the holy books that supposedly held God's word could be dispelled as ancient myths and superstitions, dried-up beliefs and narratives. God parting the Red Sea? A fairy tale no more believable than Jesus walking across wide water. But the Ten Commandments, whether handed down to Moses by God on Sinai or not, were something else. Exodus and Deuteronomy might hold different lists of commandments, the New Testament might offer different translations and enumerations of them, and the Koran might make only minimal mention of them, but still people sanctified them as guideposts in life, law, and morality.

I recall a yeshiva-trained rabbi telling me, when I was in college, that the Ten Commandments had to be studied in their hierarchical, descending order of importance. By such logic the most important commandment is the one to worship no other God but the one God, the God the Hebrews worshipped as they moved from paganism and golden calves to strict monotheism.

The next two commandments — and, according to Talmudic scholars and many other theologians, the next two most important — also evoke God. One inveighs against idol worship and the other against the misuse of God's name. Implicit in this trinity of commandments is a belief in God, a core belief in the supremacy of the one God the Hebrews believed would lead them out of Egypt and slavery to the promised land, who would protect them from their enemies by heavenly intervention. Is it any wonder that enslaved blacks in the United States would, many centuries later, identify with the exodus of those ancient Hebrews and the escape from Egyptian bondage? American slaves, too, praised God (and Jesus) and prayed fervently for deliverance and for ongoing protection from enslavement and further calamity or misfortune. Ingrained in them, as in the Hebrew flock led by Moses, was the need to exalt a higher power, one greater than what they believed they possessed. Both the Hebrew slaves in the time of Moses and the black slaves in the American South became slavishly bound to the one they saw as their creator, an almighty ruler to whom they believed they owed absolute filial piety and unceasing gratitude.

What the first commandment really discloses, above all, is mortal helplessness. One must believe in the one God absolutely, and in no other gods among the wild and abundant assortment that had long been available. All other commandments hinge on this first commandment: if people are expected to obey them, then the power behind them must be real and equipped to mete out reward and punishment. One's inability to stand against baleful and enslaving forces dictates belief in God's power. With the fear of that power comes the exalting.

As a boy I was acutely aware that many of the Hebrew prayers praised and adored God in order to express deepest gratitude to God for his blessings, out of the fear that comes with powerlessness against punishment and despair, or, perhaps above all, out of the fear of pissing off the überhegemon. The God of the Old Testament is an angry and vengeful God. Yom Kippur, the holiest day on the religious Jewish calendar, a day of profound dread and repentance, is also, more than anything else, a day to let the Almighty know how sorry we are for our mortal failures. It's a day to plead for forgiveness but also to hope that, if we are penitent enough, he will keep us and those we love alive and free from harm or evil in the year to come.

When Christians testify and accept Jesus as their Lord and savior, and when they proselytize as a way to find the true path to the kingdom of heaven for themselves, and when, from their Sunday pews, they offer praise to the divine power, they act out of their belief in a singular and infinite power that grants no quarter in its demand that there be no other God. They exalt and humble themselves before that power and confirm their helplessness and mortal dependency. Even those who presume to speak in God's name, or reckon that God's will courses through them, acknowledge God's almighty power and absolute sovereignty. God's power, or that of his only begotten carpenter son, is seen as absolute. This form of supreme exaltation is also evident in the streams of Muslims answering the call emanating from the minaret or making their way in pilgrimage to Mecca to worship and submit to Allah.

If God demands we have no other God before him, how can we not give our faith to him alone and repeatedly demonstrate to him its fullness? If salvation comes through acceptance of and obeisance to Jesus Christ, how can we not put him above all other Gods? We transgress when we do not. The annunciation heralding the birth of Christ eclipsed other annunciative moments, such as the story of Leda and the swan. The one God became a God with a better brand name in the ancient marketplace of deities.

Nietzsche's decision about God, the proclamation about the death of God by *Time* magazine's editors, and similar announcements by other mortals were all heresy, idiocy. God ruled! Jesus ruled! We of mortal flesh had to humble ourselves before immortal power. And what of those billions of

Chinese commies and godless Russians and all the others who did not embrace a code tied to God and his Ten Commandments? Confucianism, Taoism, Buddhism, Hinduism, Jainism, and Zoroastrianism are not rooted in the Abrahamic theism of Christianity, Judaism, and Islam. The Ten Commandments do not form the spine of their ethical traditions, even though much in their religious texts reflects on the same topics that are the staples of the Ten Commandments.

An agnostic is not sure about the Ten Commandments as an ethical base, because an agnostic, by definition, is a doubter. But, as the fiction writer Tobias Wolff once told me, doubt is part of faith. I considered myself a doubter, and, as the years progressed, I also saw myself as a seeker who did not want to give up believing in God. But if God existed, I wanted to know him — if not in some empirical and extrinsic way, then in a spiritual or mystical way, which is to say, an irrational or nonempirical intrinsic way. I longed for the God I had known as a boy. I longed for a certainty that, even if it lacked scientific verification, assured me of God's existence and the power behind his commandments. Couldn't I feel the presence of God without the proverbial foxhole mentality, and without the deep abiding fear that accompanies feelings of helplessness? Couldn't I peek in, even if only for a second, on the eternal, the infinite, the transcendent, the mysterious prime mover? Couldn't I do this despite my intellect, which fiercely assured me that I could not possibly know what I could not, with epistemological certainty, perceive, touch, render, or grasp? Was there a spiritual presence unrelated to the personal, concrete God of my fathers and mothers, the God of the commandments?

In my freshman year in college, when we seemed at the brink of nuclear war with the Soviet Union because of missiles

Khrushchev was shipping to Cuba, I prayed to God to keep us from nuclear incineration. While my intellect deeply doubted the efficacy of my prayer, I still wanted God to be an active and involved participant. In fear, I got down on my knees in my dormitory room while my two college roommates solemnly observed. I said aloud words I wanted to believe were heard by God, who, if he existed, surely had it within his power to keep us safe.

Back when I was still in elementary school, I had come to fear nuclear attack. My class had done duck-and-cover exercises and listened to scary talk of massive destruction and mushroom clouds and radiation from Russian MiG payloads. I knew the world was a perilous place, and that we could all, suddenly and randomly, go off in a bang, just as I knew I could meet my own end in some unforeseen, unpredictable way. God was not watching over me, my family, or my nation. Only wishful thinking and involuntary visceral responses and vestigial hope told me otherwise. Yet there I was on my knees with my two frightened college roommates, pleading with God to keep us safe. How could I be certain my prayer or the prayers of others were not being heard by a higher power? Could I depend more on what my intellect told me or what my heart longed for? A world without God seemed comfortless. Was it possible to have it both ways — to doubt God and simultaneously believe he existed?

And what of agnosticism? To even inwardly admit not knowing whether God existed directly opposed the first three commandments. Could agnosticism be a middle way between faith and disbelief, or was it simply vacillation? Could agnosticism embrace the moral views set forth in God's commandments?

I was still unwilling to call myself an agnostic. It seemed

too charged a word for a young man who fell on his knees in prayer. I could not relinquish the first three, and possibly the most vital, of the Ten Commandments. Years later I would interview atheists such as Christopher Hitchens, Sam Harris, and Richard Dawkins, whose observations would not dissuade me from recognizing that I could not, with certainty, know of God's existence or nonexistence, especially not with the kind of certainty that marked both deep faith and the cocksure atheism that negated faith. If God existed, how could I possibly know what he was capable of?

The problem with the atheists I encountered was that they all seemed so certain that God did not and could not exist. Paradoxically, they resembled fundamentalists in their atheism — even though Dawkins spoke almost glowingly of the beauty of nature and Hitchens of his attraction to the idea of the numinous, telling me how his friend, the British novelist Ian McEwan, had given him a greater conceptual understanding of it. A self-proclaimed lifetime contrarian, Hitchens had taken on God. His book title said it all — *God Is Not Great*. But how could he, or anyone, know? He and many other atheists, it seemed to me, were thinking of the traditional, anthropomorphic God tied to religion's dark history, the celestial big daddy whom religious zealots killed for and over, the God who would punish boys if they masturbated and girls if they lost their maidenheads.

Chapter 3

THE TEN COMMANDMENTS
AND A CODE OF ONE'S OWN

s a college student, I decided I could create my own set of commandments. I had read all of Ernest Hemingway and realized that, in spite of the nihilistic view found in his powerful short stories and his novels such as *A Farewell to Arms* and *The Sun Also Rises*, there was an appealing code. At least it appealed to me. Or, I should say, parts of it did. Despite all the blustering machismo and small-minded prejudices in his work, the Hemingway code was rooted both in the idea of showing grace under pressure and in acting in a manly and stoic way in the face of adversity and accepting an existential reality that precluded faith. Though Hemingway exalted the Catholicism he was born into and influenced by, he nevertheless accepted the notion that existence preceded essence, that we create who we are by our choices and actions despite a deterministic universe and regardless of what we are born with, or what, my mother would insist, was ladled out to us by God.

Hemingway also believed one could be drawn into a nearly communal ethos with others who were like one in spirit and sensibility, into the he-or-she-is-one-of-us ethic. When, in *The Sun Also Rises*, Brett Ashley in effect releases the young bullfighter Romero from her hold, she tells Jake Barnes it's what they have instead of God. Jakes replies, "Some people have God.... Quite a lot." Brett says then, "He never worked very well with me," and Jake responds by suggesting they have another martini. In Hemingway's world we are connected to those we like, and who are like us, by pleasures such as liquor and a stoic view of life, by a code and commitment to a life of action, by a belief in a here and now without frills. Life is a quest for transient pleasure and courage, where we must accept the one and only predetermined certainty — our fragile mortality.

Other writers too — philosophers and poets — provided me with a tentative and evolving blueprint as I planted myself in the world of ideas and embraced the life of the mind. Albert Camus especially affected me with his notion that the only valid philosophical question was whether to commit suicide. The quest for knowledge itself became an integral part of my developing code, and I absorbed as much as I could from great writers, philosophers, and poets. If I was to have a higher purpose or a sudden blitzkrieg of faith, it would have to enter without being wished for. It would have to be genuine, convincing. I continued to long for that kind of certainty, a certainty that I knew only a form of spiritual sustenance could provide. But in the meantime I settled on the idea of developing a code based on my Jewish cultural traditions and on what I derived from the writers, like Hemingway, and existentialist thinkers, like Camus, that I was intellectually drawn to and who believed in the power of the human will. I was convinced, by the age of nineteen, that once death arrived, it meant the end of consciousness, the big and lasting sleep.

I came remarkably close to dying, in fact, in a speeding car driven by a liquor-swigging fellow student named Dave, who lost control one night on a slick wintry Ohio turnpike as a giant rig bore down on us. It was astonishing how narrowly we escaped death's jaws. I saw the truck's lights glaring directly at me and was sure my life was about to end — until I realized we'd skidded off the road and flopped into a huge snowdrift on the side of the turnpike, which had only recently been plowed. I crawled out first and stood watching as Dave rushed out of the driver's seat and buried his flask in the high snow that had miraculously cushioned his car. He then fell to the ground and kissed it.

In the instant when I had stared into the truck's lights and believed my doom was sealed, I had thought that I, at nineteen, would barely have an obituary. A sentence or two would sum up my life. It seemed as if the experience of coming so perilously close to death should have set off in me a charge for God, gratitude for life and for having suffered no physical harm. But by that point, only a year after the Cuban missile crisis had knocked me to my knees, something had shifted.

I was more of an agnostic at this time, although I still couldn't fully embrace the word. Standing in the snow I thanked God for saving me from collision with the rig, but I did it in a mealymouthed, automatic way. I was certain that, had I been killed, I would not have entered an afterlife. My doubts about such concepts as an afterlife had become too strong, stronger than my previous willingness to accept the comforting notion of a life or form of ongoing consciousness after death, some soul transmigration or ascent of the soul to a higher reward or descent to punishment. I was with Dylan Thomas on this: "After the first death there is no other."

Nevertheless, belief in God was another matter. Faith-based existentialists like Søren Kierkegaard and Martin Buber, and great thinkers such as Friedrich Nietzsche and Jean-Paul Sartre who denied the existence of a higher power, had already imprinted me with their ideas, as had poets like Thomas and a myriad of other writers and thinkers I greedily ingested. All of them had contributed to the life philosophy I was formulating. Ideas had begun to percolate in me, assisted by my ambitious reading and my desire to form a code that fit my personal, evolving brand of agnosticism. This code recognized no afterlife, no involvement by God in human affairs, and included my own doubts about God and the Ten Commandments. It wasn't that I found anything objectionable about the Ten Commandments or about making them the guideposts for my life. But the first four were connected intimately to a God I had come to question, and the other six seemed too absolute. A code birthed in agnosticism, I was beginning to realize, had little relationship to absolutes.

I had been troubled early on by the absoluteness of the prohibitions in the Ten Commandments. Even as a boy I had doubted that the commandment not to kill fit every instance. Did it really apply to battle or to self-defense? Was it all right to kill a figure like Hitler or Stalin to prevent mass slaughter of others? What about the killing done by the state in response to heinous crimes? And what about the killing of animals?

These questions provided fodder for late-night adolescent debates, and for later discussions that would metamorphose into more serious and weighty moral analysis. They are the questions of one who questions. They can lead, ultimately, to confusion and indecision, even to the comedic. Was there,

I asked my students decades later in a literature class I was teaching, an ethical imperative not to eat meat because to do so meant animals had to be killed? Plants at the time were being heralded as living creatures that supposedly exhibited responses to human touch and sound. They were, at any rate, life-forms, and they too had to be killed if humans were to eat. One could, I noted to my class, limit one's diet to fruit, but that would mean complicity in abortion. So, I concluded, to be absolutely moral, one had to not eat.

And what of the absoluteness of the commandment not to steal? You cannot read Victor Hugo's *Les Miserables* without recognizing the injustice done to poor Jean Valjean when he is forced to serve nineteen years in jail for stealing a loaf of bread to survive. And yet, we were commanded by the highest power never to steal. How absolute was that commandment? Or, for that matter, any commandment?

As a kid I took the commandment against stealing seriously and refused to go along with my pals who urged me to be their partner in swiping clothes from Cleveland's May Company or cigarettes from the corner pharmacy. "Klepto," I called one kid who seemed to take inordinate pride in what he could steal. He was cunning enough to get away with a lot of petty heists. Why, I wondered, wasn't he being punished? I chummed around for a while with another guy, whom we called Jake the Thief. I thought he was a colorful character, and he went out of his way to win my approval, which flattered my boyish ego. But we all knew he stole things from people's homes, even the homes of his supposed friends and neighbors. My dad put it best one day when he said to me of Jake: "Your friend has larceny in his heart." And Jake, whose father was a bookie, predictably found himself, as the years progressed, in serious trouble for check forgery, trouble that he managed somehow to weasel out of. What, I wondered after Jake's arrest, would be the ultimate punishment for all his theft?

Jews did not seem to believe in hell, really, and I certainly didn't, so where or how would punishment for theft occur if not on earth? And what of those who, like Jean Valjean, stole out of desperation? Were there exceptions to the commandment? Mitigating circumstances? Get-out-of-violating-the-commandment-free cards? I raised such questions inwardly, and they sounded to me even then a lot like Philosophy 101. They suggested, as I continued to grapple with them in college, that I might need to join what by then were the growing ranks of secular humanists, who were vilified for holding views tantamount to moral relativism. Yet how could one be absolutist about any of the commandments five through ten? I loved my parents and felt the value of the commandment to honor them. But I knew there were abusive and dishonorable parents who deserved no honor. Parents who were cruel to small children deserved punishment. In fact I felt outraged enough about violence against children that in such cases, were I guaranteed immunity, I could possibly have personally violated the commandment not to kill.

If the commandments were listed in order of importance, how could the one obligating us to rest on the Sabbath be more important than those forbidding us to steal or kill or the one commanding us to honor our parents? The holiness attached to the idea of keeping the Sabbath is allied with the belief that creation was completed in six days and, therefore, like the first three commandments, fundamentally tied to belief in God and his filling a short-term work order. This commandment is viewed as absolute by many Orthodox Jews, who, believing they must rest on the day of rest, refuse to drive, answer the telephone, push a button on an elevator, or even flush a toilet.

I knew Jews like that when I was growing up, including some of my neighbors. They refused to do anything other than walk to and from the Orthodox synagogue they could not afford to join. An itinerant freelance rabbi named Katz (my friends and I called him Rabbi Katzintoochas, meaning "Rabbi Katz in the ass") taught haftarah bar mitzvah preparation to their kids and others whose families couldn't afford to join a synagogue. Rabbi Katzintoochas would park blocks away on Saturday and slink over to the home of those he was teaching haftarah that day, to avoid being seen driving his car on Shabbat. This was during the days when I would play hooky from Sabbath school on Saturdays. One Saturday my friend Froggy and I got into the rabbi's unlocked car and stayed crouched down until he furtively made it back to where the car was parked. When he opened the door, we sprang up immediately and shouted in unison: "Good *shabbus*, Rabbi!" I honestly feared Katzintoochas was going to die of cardiac arrest.

My point is that absolutism leads too often to hypocrisy, but also to rigidity and fanaticism. In many cases, it leads directly to religious fundamentalism, which — as writers like the ex-nun Karen Armstrong, author of *The Battle for God: A History of Fundamentalism*, have shown — can breed murderous acts. During humankind's time on this planet, there has been far too much absolutism, and far too much absolutism remains the global order of the day. But there has also been, believers will argue, too many exemptions from the commandments, too much sliding away from the requirement to follow the will of God as set forth to Moses on Sinai, too much moral relativism.

Can one say that adultery should absolutely never be committed? Poor Edna Pontellier in Kate Chopin's *The Awakening*, impelled by desire she could not understand and a maddening search for fulfillment. Or Gustave Flaubert's Emma Bovary or Leo Tolstoy's Anna Karenina. Literature had the unsettling effect of expanding my empathy for fallen women, who defied God's seventh commandment. How could one not empathize with Anton Chekhov's sweet, tortured, religious Anna, married to a flunky, or with men like her lover, Dmitri Gurov, whose wife was hard and unyielding, the chief characters in the magnificent love story "The Lady with the Dog," which Vladimir Nabokov called one of the greatest stories ever written?

And what about Theodore Dreiser's George Hurstwood, in *Sister Carrie*, who is both an adulterer and a thief? He feels compelled to steal from the safe of the company he works for so he can run away from his stultifying bourgeois life and his cold and materialistic wife, Julia, and find a life of love with the vital, fresh-faced Carrie Meeber. Hurstwood winds up a lost vagrant, but the point is that we feel empathy for him as we do for Willa Cather's effeminate and foppish Paul in her classic story "Paul's Case," the story of a young boy who, like Hurstwood, is driven to steal. Paul wants to escape the dull, severe Calvinism of his boyhood home and the neighborhood with the odd Shakespearean name of Cordelia Street, where all the boys are brought up to be the same. Paul knows he is different. He, too, meets a terrible fate, throwing himself in front of an oncoming train rather than going back to the intolerable psychological oppression of his school and Cordelia Street and his motherless home. The real questions we must ask about transgressions such as adultery and theft are: when should empathy override the absoluteness of the commandments, and when should mercy override justice?

Literary characters helped subvert my sense that the commandments were absolute and provided me with a greater understanding of the wide and complex range of humanity and its frailties. This in turn increased my empathy, which I was obliged to fold into my evolving personal code. Empathy did not mean allowing, or making ready excuses for, moral transgressions, but it did mean one had to determine the nature of transgressions and their often moral complexity. One had to wrestle with what was right and what was not — as well as with the more formidable moral question of good and evil.

Hester Prynne, for example, is the adulterous wife of Roger Chillingworth in Nathaniel Hawthorne's classic *The Scarlet Letter*, and Chillingworth is a man whom Hawthorne makes us see as evil. Hester, whom Hawthorne compares to the before-her-time Puritan-era feminist and banished heretic Anne Hutchinson, is drawn into adultery with the Reverend Arthur Dimmesdale, who tells her their adultery has a sanctity of its own. It might be difficult, as D. H. Lawrence has suggested, to imagine those two at it in the woods, because Dimmesdale is so fraught with pained asceticism. But given Roger Chillingworth's evil nature and Hester's humanity and vitality, one understands her violation of the commandment that ultimately condemns her to wear the ignominious letter.

We realize that Hawthorne is dramatizing in *The Scarlet Letter* the shocking and heretical notion that people are in wretched and abusive marriages that make them capable of falling in love with, or making love with, others. There is also, in the character of Hester Prynne, Hawthorne's idea of the negative path, of Hester personally gaining greater empathy and a more profound understanding of her own humanity and the humanity of others because of her violation of the commandment and the punishment she endures. She becomes nobler than all the religious Puritans who condemn her and turn her into a pariah.

As long as marriage exists, adultery will be seen as a sin, because marriage, like the Ten Commandments, has been tied to belief in God, even though marriage wasn't much of a religious phenomenon before Christendom, and specifically Catholicism, linked it to the church and made it a sacrament. According to feminist scholar Marilyn Yalom, the Greeks and the Hebrews saw marriage as a contract, similar to a promissory note today, with concomitant civil or financial consequences if broken. Yalom says marriage had the imprimatur of the gods in ancient Greece and Rome but was by no means an irreversible affair since divorce was permitted in the ancient world and even common in Rome.

In a number of states in this country, including New York and Florida, adultery and physical cruelty were for many years the only grounds for divorce. Now adultery, in the non-sharia West, appears nearly commonplace. A long-running syndicated reality television show called *Cheaters* catches the unfaithful, both married and unmarried, with hidden cameras, and the episodes turn into confrontations between the cuckolded and the faithless. And it seems as if almost every day some political figure, too, is exposed as an adulterer. These would-be public servants may aspire to nobler ideals, but they succumb to transgression, the word adopted by Tiger Woods following his notorious car accident that apparently was tied to an argument with his wife over his adultery.

Even popular attitudes toward adultery have changed with the times, as television and film no longer make it de rigueur for an adulterer, especially a woman, to wind up dead. And in the real world, both the Prince of Wales and John McCain had adulterous relationships without ever being much stigmatized for it. Britain has become, for the most part, a nation of nonworshippers, and morality in the United States has changed exponentially despite the high percentage of those who call themselves religious. Ronald Reagan was the first U.S. president who rose to the Oval Office with a divorce in his personal history, which would have been morally unacceptable only a decade earlier. Morality and religion are not necessarily mutually bound, but the weakening of the force of the commandments has made them less viable and has also strengthened religious fundamentalism and the inevitable hypocrisy and absolutism it breeds.

The first four commandments are tied to God, the last four to property. Theft and adultery — both essentially crimes against property, since marriage was viewed as a form of ownership — were prohibited for the same reasons as bearing false witness and coveting what belonged, or was seen as belonging, to another. All four are clearly about possession and ownership, and the prohibition against adultery is also about keeping vows and ensuring that men do not abandon their wives and offspring. Though the stricture against bearing false witness has often been seen in a broader context as a prohibition against lying or mendacity, the commandment historically has been tied to notions of property and ownership. And how absolute can one expect to be on the subject of lying, even on lying while under an oath to God? My mother, who believed God marked down every single lie in a big book, still liked to emphasize that there were differences between big and small lies, even so-called white lies calculated to keep someone's feelings from being hurt. Not coveting what another possesses might be the most vexing commandment of the final four, since coveting seems almost an intrinsic part of human nature.

I had a religious-minded Catholic crony in high school named Wayne, who was aching with lust for his neighbor

Jerry's blonde, big-busted wife. Wayne confessed to me one day that he regularly masturbated, sometimes two or three times a day, while thinking about her. He also revealed that he simply couldn't get over the fact that Jerry was a jerk to his wife, mean and bossy, unable to appreciate her sirenlike appeal the way covetous Wayne did. Wayne was fearful God would punish him for coveting his neighbor's wife. He told me he confessed to his priest and actually asked the priest if this meant a place in hell would be reserved for him, and whether jerking off so much to her image could make him lose his sperm supply. He had heard somewhere that the Bible warned that a man only had what he described to me as "a thousand loads."

Murder remains for many the central commandment despite its position at number 6, and despite all the murders that God, if he is truly omnipotent or involved in human affairs, is complicit in or simply uninvolved. The greatest moral seriousness is still attached to murder, especially premeditated murder, which is one reason why it is so often popularly dramatized. The sixth commandment has the greatest currency even though the world is awash in murder. Most who believe in God accept prima facie that God, regardless of how we reckon with his inscrutable nature, does not countenance murder, even though God himself has been given a James Bond–style license to kill by his true believers, who frequently also give themselves license to kill in his name.

If higher intelligence manifests directly in our lives, one has to reckon with the kill toll, and especially with the number who die horribly and for no reason, or by the hands of others in God's name. But behind the sixth commandment, and anchored to its ongoing power over us, is the value attached to the preciousness of human life. Why human life should be more important than other animal life is a question I leave to philosophers like Peter Singer and others who argue that perhaps it shouldn't. But spiritual seekers, and hordes of the secular minded, and those of little or no faith all still confirm the sacredness of human life and the tradition that has come down to us from the sixth commandment. Even atheists speak of the sanctity of human life.

Yet if one assumes that God directs or intervenes — the God most people believe in and worship, the God who supposedly commands us not to kill — he can perhaps be seen as the greatest and most random of killers, one for whom murder is an ongoing specialty. He is the one in whose name fervent believers have for centuries killed. This same God, the faithful would quickly argue, grants us life and all the wonders and joys of the planet — even though the planet may be, without any guarantee of divine intervention, perilously close to nuclear annihilation or ecologic catastrophe or asteroids or staggering losses of precious human life from a yet-to-be anticipated pandemic. That same God instills in us, according to believers, all that is holy, good, and true and grants us life everlasting, while nonbelievers cede none of this and do not attribute our virtues or strengths or good health or good fortune to God.

The great twentieth-century novel and short story writer Flannery O'Connor, as devout a Catholic in her daily life as most pontiffs or priests, created one of literature's first mass killers, the Misfit, in her most famous and widely taught story, "A Good Man Is Hard to Find." The Misfit kills people randomly, an entire family in fact, but he broods over theological questions such as whether Jesus actually raised the dead. His words to the grandmother, a foolish old lady he is about to shoot to death, hearken back to those of Ivan Karamazov in *The Brothers Karamazov*, who says that anything is permissible in a world without God. Had he been there to see Jesus raise the dead, the Misfit says to the grandmother, he would have known. Since he was not there he cannot know, and so he might as well kill people.

Was the main problem of the past century, as W. E. B. DuBois, the author of *The Souls of Black Folk*, famously proclaimed, "the problem of the color line"? Or was it what Flannery O'Connor recognized as finding God and knowing what God was capable of performing or allowing, and knowing whether he was in his heaven or in our lives? I'm left, like the Misfit, with the inability to know, but I lack the desire to succumb to what I see as the evil in a code like his — one in which there is no stricture against killing or doing mean things. Speaking of Jesus as the only one who raised the dead, the Misfit tells the grandmother: "If He did what He said, then it's nothing for you to do but throw away everything and follow Him, and if He didn't, then it's nothing for you to do but enjoy the few minutes you got left the best you can by killing somebody or burning down his house or doing some other meanness to him."

I can offer no good reason why killing (or any other form of meanness) is not permissible, other than the importance of adhering to human-made laws or to one's own code. The Misfit wished he could have been there to see Jesus raise the dead, and I wish I could know whether God really handed commandments to Moses on Mount Sinai. The real challenge of hewing to the particulars of one's own code is to stand behind it in times that require courage and in moments that put life and death on the line.

In *Crime and Punishment*, Fyodor Dostoyevsky's character Raskolnikov makes philosophic attempts to be a Nietzschean superman and kill, without conscience, his old landlady. From this, we have come, in the United States, to an age of the Misfit and an age in which the moral weight of murder has diminished. Mass murder and serial killing especially have become a significant part of American life and popular culture, and subjects of philosophical meditations on evil and a world without the moral force of God. In the past few decades, so many infamous figures have been identified with serial killing that someone produced a collection of serial-killer playing cards — featuring the likes of John Wayne Gacy, David Berkowitz, Richard Ramirez, Ted Bundy, members of the Manson family, and other representatives of mayhem — apparently worth collecting like the traditional bubblegum cards of my youth.

I knew we had crossed a Rubicon in America in 1991 when *Silence of the Lambs*, a Jonathan Demme film about not one but two serial killers, won five Academy Awards, including Best Picture and Best Actor, given to Anthony Hopkins for his chilling performance as Hannibal Lecter. In 2007 Javier Bardem won an Oscar for his equally frightening portrayal of a serial killer in the Coen brothers' film version of Cormac McCarthy's novel *No Country for Old Men*. The idea of an entire family senselessly murdered was still horrific new fictional territory when Flannery O'Connor's famous story was published in 1955. And that shock factor was still powerful a decade later when Truman Capote published *In Cold Blood* about the real-life murders of the Clutter family in Holcomb, Kansas.

We in the West are not yet desensitized to murder in any way remotely comparable to that in parts of Africa and in the Middle East, where ongoing carnage suggests that life is intolerably cheap. But we have become, thanks to a glut of media murder portrayals, increasingly inured to the kind of killings that once precipitated great shock throughout the land — Charles Whitman in his University of Texas tower shooting innocents like ducks in an amusement park, or Charles Starkweather and his childhood companion, Caril Ann Fugate, murdering indiscriminately throughout the Midwest in a spree that would later be immortalized in the movies *Badlands* and *Natural Born Killers,* and in Bruce Springsteen's "Nebraska."

Popular culture has continued to ratchet up the thrill kill numbers in films, and society has become used to daily feedings — via magazines, newspapers, tabloids, and television newscasts — of homicides, serial and mass murders, and senseless mayhem, along with the glut of television shows about crime scene investigations. One longs for restoration of the sixth commandment to people's minds, rather than to watch a population become more and more desensitized to the moral force of that commandment's prohibition against murder. If God's concern about murder necessitated the sixth commandment, what are we to make of the remorseless and psychopathic killings in the world or, for that matter, the spate of fictional killings that Americans seem to feast on that have made murder a kind of meme?

I've heard normally good-hearted, decent people who have been emotionally wounded by a spouse, or enraged at the treatment of one of their children, or financially crippled by deceit, speak seriously about wanting to hire a hit man. Where is God in all this? What exactly is his role? I take up these questions in the next chapter, but here I'll say that, if one is uncertain of him or his involvement, or if one doubts the absoluteness of his thou-shalt-not commandments, then perhaps one is obliged to create a code of one's own or a different conceptual rendering of Almighty God. Isn't that what family members or compassionate caregivers must do when they opt for euthanasia rather than ongoing suffering, in spite of how they may feel about the absoluteness of the commandment against murder?

The late comedian George Carlin had a riff in which he talked about our not needing the first four commandments and the desirability of combining the rest of the commandments to reduce their number. He irreverently called the commandments "bullshit," a political and religious marketing ploy designed to control people, whom he dismissed as being mostly stupid. He then whittled the number of commandments down from ten to two: be honest and faithful, and don't kill anyone. Or at least, try not to kill anyone. He pointed out that the devoutly religious seemed to be the ones most capable of killing, and, of course, they do so in the name of God.

Moreover, Carlin thought that not coveting was stupid, since coveting goods keeps the economy going. As for honoring one's parents with obedience and respect, he said obedience and respect had to be earned and should be based on the parents' performance. Carlin's routine is a potent mix of rhetorical observation combined with the cleverness of a comic who loved being iconoclastic and broke from his Catholic upbringing. In fact, Carlin made it sound as though God had nothing to do with the commandments. Hustlers cooked them up, according to Carlin, and decided on ten because of its strength as a number in the decimal system and its relevance to things such as decades and top-ten lists.

It is highly likely that the Ten Commandments came from human beings, rather than God, and that each of the three different versions that appear in the Bible was written by the presumed author of the book in which it is found. Some, however, assume that humanity's greatest ethical code may have originated in Egyptian or Hittite writings. Regardless of its origins, one still has to ask whether there could have been a guiding hand, a supernal force, behind the commandments. The answer: We don't know. Or at least, I certainly don't know.

Those who believe in the absoluteness of the commandments cannot create a slippery slope of circumstances that might allow for certain violations. Instead of tying myself in a knot trying to negotiate the absolutism of the Ten Commandments, or simply becoming a card-carrying secular humanist, I elected, in college, to remain in doubt about both God and his stone tablets. There were simply too many necessary exemptions. Prohibitions against bearing false witness and coveting were especially difficult to establish as absolute. I recall one of my young students, in an all-too-revealing display of our shifting moral sands, discussing the Ten Commandments with me and saying, with absolute seriousness, "I know we're not supposed to covet our neighbor's wife, Dr. Krasny. But what if our neighbor's wife is hot and wants to hook up?"

Why did I decide not to go with what my ancestors went with (if they were my ancestors ...), a code that has endured for centuries and continues to have the respect of even nonbelievers who have deleted God from their mental hard drive? Surely it wasn't a weakness to take the Decalogue as inherited wisdom? The simple, unvarnished truth is, I wanted my own set of commandments, my own ethical code, my own personal morality, my own certainty, if I could find it, without the necessity of a divinely prescribed moral platform. But why? Why not stumble through life without any steadfast commandments at all, living as many others do, devoid of divine rules?

A credo for life could simply be an agnostic credo — call it an agnostic's obbligato. I could spend a lifetime vacillating, seeking, fluctuating, and moving between momentary and ever-changing certainties and doubts — call them life's antipodes — between belief in nothing and belief in something, a dialectic with no terminus or synthesis, just like Samuel Beckett's *Waiting for Godot*, with its two acts of waiting for the mysterious and unseen Godot, who never manifests. In *Waiting for Godot* there is no third act, only the play's two tramps floating upright in an anarchic sea of nothingness. Was that what some of the religious folk vilified as moral relativism? Morality, it seemed to me, could be strong and resilient and in flux without being relative or absolute. Theories of post-structuralism and the Gallic musings of Jacques Derrida, Michel Foucault, Julia Kristeva, and Roland Barthes would usher into my head that era's zeitgeist, the certainty of uncertainty, itself another absolute. I felt myself shifting, in some new form of agnostic dualism, between the certainty of uncertainty and the uncertainty of uncertainty.

I could, I knew, try to keep the commandments in my own way, and I could draw on an ethical code of my own. Such a code of personal commandments began to take shape in my mind and centered on ideas of trying to be truthful and honest and civil and kind and humane in all my dealings with others, and on accepting my own existential limitations. Perhaps the work that had the most effect on me at that point was *Waiting for Godot*, which spoke poignantly of the human condition and the existential dilemma we all face, as well as of a transcendent force that can be a raison d'être and a harbinger of hope and purpose, and yet never be seen or met or known. Beckett denied that Godot stood for God, even a diminutive one like that suggested by the two additional letters. Yet it is hard to escape the feeling of agnosticism conveyed by the play.

Agnostics wait. But more important, agnostics need to find a way to fill time and amuse and entertain and invent for themselves while waiting for a higher authority or higher meaning that may not arrive. Like the two Beckett clochards Vladimir and Estragon, we all need to establish a code of some sort that can at least keep us in the game. The time-filling activities of Beckett's two protagonists are, for the most part, trivial and inconsequential and replete with frivolous language play. But this seems to be a good deal of what Beckett wants to point out to us about the human condition. As Joan Didion's character Maria Wyeth, in the famous Hollywood novel *Play It as It Lays*, discovered, you either opt out of the game or you stay in. Camus instilled in me the notion that there is no question more essential than whether to stay in the game or withdraw voluntarily. It seemed only sensible, therefore, for one who elected to stay to find a code, a workable, if not adjustable, and nonabsolute paradigm.

It was Hemingway and Beckett and Camus, as well as Nathaniel Hawthorne and Martin Buber and T. S. Eliot and Saul Bellow and basic classic teachings from antiquity, such as the golden and silver rules, that propelled me to establish a code of my own. It seemed axiomatic that much of the distilled wisdom in the major religions, and in the works of great writers and thinkers, who at that point in my life seemed to nearly all be men, had to do with loving and caring for other human beings, trying to do good deeds, and if possible, giving of oneself. I couldn't love my neighbor (his stereo was too loud and his body odor too acrid), but I could act respectfully and show kindness until or unless neither worked and I was provoked to act otherwise.

There was no heaven-sent reason to show others kindness and respect, especially those who seemed ill deserving. It would not ensure me a place with the angels or assure approbation from an invisible deity. But I felt that by acting with respect and kindness I was doing something pragmatic that would not only serve my nature but also my desire to be liked and get kindness and respect in return. I could reinforce my decision by telling myself, in ways that Bellow had seeded in my thinking, that I was seeking to be a good man, a mensch, endeavoring to act with rectitude, seeking to live in truth or at least seeking my own truth without harming or hurting unless provoked.

Spurred on by a course taught by a wonderful professor and T. S. Eliot scholar named Eric Thompson, I decided that, for me, a principal thou-shalt-not would be not to treat people as objects but to strive for what Martin Buber brilliantly identified as I-Thou relationships, in which one spoke ontologically, with one's entire being. This was a challenging personal commandment, and, like the commandments from Sinai, it was not absolute.

Avoiding objectification of young women was especially challenging. I was an overly libidinal young man in those prefeminist days, which the comic Lily Tomlin called "the decade of foreplay." I was on the make. The male code I absorbed from those around me, particularly my guy friends, was a Don Juan–Hugh Hefner code contrary to the higher-minded, Martin Buber–based one that was also forming in my mind. The guy code was more like what a sleazy guy in my neighborhood we called Slimy Hymie described, when we were kids, as the goals of the Four F Club: find them, feel them, fuck them, and forget them. During my adolescence, *Playboy* magazine was a major influence. I avidly read Hugh Hefner's philosophy, a manifesto on what it meant to take up a hedonistic way of life tied to a notches-on-the-headboard ideal that would become identified a generation later with the figure of the player.

I liked girls and I liked sex, and I liked the feeling of conquest that came with what we then called "getting girls." But it
was all terribly confusing, because there were girls I could get
and girls I could not get, and did getting a girl for the sake of sex
mean I was taking advantage of her or objectifying her? Being a
would-be rake seemed cool even though also predatory, but the
newer wave of feminism that would insist on not objectifying
women — and eventually on full sexual equality — and throw
everything out of whack had not yet begun to lap at young
men like me. As long as I didn't take someone against her will,
I thought, whom was I hurting? And I told myself that I had
been hurt by what I saw as unrequited love, by young women
who had flat-out rejected me. Codes in conflict!

Sometimes, mostly because of my own insecurities, and in
accordance with what Harvard psychologist William Pollack
aptly calls "the boy's code," I would be cruel or aggressive,
would ridicule and make fun of people, but I would also feel
defensive and insecure about my masculinity. I wanted to follow the commandment I had given myself not to objectify
other human beings, not to see them as separate from their
humanity. Thou shalt not hurt or objectify others seemed a
sound, sensible commandment for me to follow scrupulously.
But I found I was capable of mischief, of unwittingly hurting
others or hurting them out of carelessness or out of the adolescent glee that came from putting others down. Moreover
I could not be saintly or pacific, both noble ideals, because
I was driven by another code rooted in my boyhood and in
American film culture. This one could be whittled down to
the idea that, if someone messed with me, I would mess with
him or her in return.

It didn't matter that I fed myself one of my mother's favorite platitudes — that two wrongs don't make a right —

whenever I felt hurt or mistreated, rejected or disrespected. I wanted payback, which seemed appropriate when someone did me wrong. There was nothing philosophically high-minded about such feelings, but they were undeniable. If God or the universe wasn't going to mete out punishment to others who screwed me over, or who screwed over the people I cared about, then I had to step up. This was principle. It was fairness. It was justice. I discovered, of course, that such thinking can be self-aggrandizing, not to mention self-endangering and self-defeating. Or just vainglorious, as in an episode with Andy S., though in that case I did manage to keep another commandment I had fashioned for myself — I kept my word.

Fast-forward. I'm a PhD student at the University of Wisconsin. I'm months away from leaving Madison for San Francisco, and I'm living with my girlfriend and future wife in an off-campus apartment. Andy S., a neighbor down the hall and a compulsive dope smoker who lives with his girlfriend, Cheryl, suggests we engage in a couple swap. I politely decline. A number of weeks later, I finish my class miles away from the apartment I rent on campus. I go to my car, open the door, and get in. All the knobs on the car's dashboard have been removed, as has the lighter and ashtray. The seat belt is fastened across the steering wheel. I find this bizarre and perplexing, and I phone in a report to the police. Then I drive back to the apartment and park for the night. The next morning, I discover that all the items purloined the day before are back in place.

Around the time of this incident I also notice profane graffiti spray-painted on the wall outside my apartment, and I receive a couple of weird, incoherent late-night phone calls. It all seems to add up to menace. I buy a handgun. I'm not enthusiastic about the idea of owning a handgun, but I had been reading Malcolm X and Franz Fanon and, as usual, was strongly influenced by what I was reading. Turning the other cheek was not part of my morphing personal code. If some potentially malignant force was out there and was after me, I would be prepared. I related all this to Andy and a couple of other neighbors. Andy took it all in and asked incredulously, "You really bought a gun?"

Months later, only days before I was to leave for San Francisco, I learned that all of what had occurred had been done by Andy. A stoned Andy apologetically informed me of this and said he had simply been playing pranks on me. He had intended to tell me everything, but had become afraid once I purchased the gun. I thanked him for his truthfulness and assured him that, in telling me, he had done the right thing. But I also told him that it was my code to do something back. I would have to even the score. We shook hands and I thanked him again for coming clean. I had not the faintest idea what I would do as payback, but as often happens when opportunity and imagination meet, I came up with what seemed like the proper action.

A thug who drove a big Harley motorcycle periodically visited a young woman in one of the apartments on our floor, a not-too-bright beautician named Meg. She had two Chihuahuas, named Mañana and Tortilla, and this beau of hers, who looked like a motorcycle gang member, was often drunk and unruly and had on at least one occasion, it was reported to me by another neighbor, punched one of Meg's Chihuahuas. I had had an unpleasant exchange of words with this character one night over his disorderliness and had sized him up then as a sot and a brute. After my talk with Andy, I noticed that the thug's motorcycle was parked in the apartment drive, and on it I left the following note: "I live in apartment 23B. My name is Andy S. I bashed into your Harley."

I was tempted to add "tough shit" but decided against it. Vainglorious? Yes. But I had kept my word and had, in my own mind at least, evened the score. I was, I told myself, being true to my personal code. It didn't even matter to me that I didn't know what transpired between Andy and the thug. (I do know, however, that Andy lives and thrives!)

Thou shalt not be rude or discourteous also seemed a worthy and ennobling commandment to follow. I was drawn to acting with civility and gentlemanly affability, provided there were no scores to be evened. Civility and gentlemanly affability were, in my mind, strongly linked to not objectifying others. But civility posed a problem when I was confronted by rudeness or, worse, what I took to be lack of respect for me personally or someone I cared about. And to what extent was I supposed to follow a code of gentlemanly affability when faced with manifold human discourtesy, stupidity, and cruelty?

With the long, hippie hair I had as a PhD student, I could incite others simply by my appearance and did so one day in a 7-11. A Wisconsin good old boy in hunting attire pointed me out to his buddy and fellow hunter. "Hey, Clyde," he said, "is it a guy or a girl? Why don't we pull its pants down and see if it's got a dink." I let the moment pass and stared malevolently at the guy as he paid for his goods and left the store. I felt every muscle in my body tighten, and I realized I was ready to fight, almost hoping for the opportunity to prove my strength and manhood. How foolish to be ready to fight over words, to not forgive ignorance, but how red-blooded American to want to kick ass.

Thou shalt do good deeds was another of my personal

commandments. Sometimes this one was difficult to obey because my temper was short or others didn't seem to deserve even common kindness. I wanted to do good, to be a *mensch*, but what did it mean to do good, and how could I know whether my motives were good or I simply wanted to feel good about myself, to be well thought of? And did it matter?

I wanted to think that good deeds were tethered to *rachmones*, the Jewish compassion for those less fortunate, or to *tsaddaka*, the ideal of charity. But how to turn *rachmones* and *tsaddaka* into real deeds was a basic challenge, since I also dearly wanted to avoid being made a sucker. Charity seemed the noblest of virtues, but the great Jewish philosopher Maimonides pointed out that the highest form of charity derived from an absence of egoistic desire and an absence of hope that others would recognize one's charitable deeds. How was it possible to eliminate such motives? Well, what about the case of Sir Nicholas Winton, who set up a rescue operation in Prague in 1938? He was a twenty-nine-year-old London stockbroker who personally saved the lives of hundreds of mostly Jewish children by finding funds for their transport to safety and for their repatriation or foster care. He told no one. Not even his wife, Grete, knew of his heroic deeds until 1988, when she discovered a scrapbook of old correspondence he had kept.

I went one day, as an undergraduate, with a group of fraternity brothers to an orphanage and spent an afternoon playing with and giving piggyback rides to orphans. I left feeling good about what I'd done and about myself, but I also reflected that the Polaroids taken of me with various orphans on my back would come in handy to show girls what a swell guy I was. I wondered, though, how genuine such acts could be if they were done partly because of a need for the approval of oneself or others. Was intention immaterial? Should my code be dictated by circumstance, and should it shift according to need or desire? I was forming a code but had serious doubt even about shaping a code, especially one that could come close to being absolute or pure. But I was also trying to lay claim to my own commandments, my own guideposts, ones whose source and moral force was not the God I had lost but the one I still hoped to find.

Chapter 4

WHERE IS GOD?
More on Codes and God's Place in Mine

Trying to fashion a personal code from a crazy quilt of different readings and perceptions and experiences and feelings presented far more challenges than simply following the Ten Commandments. My heritage I considered Hebraic, despite Koestler's notion that Russian Jews like me were descended from the Khazars. I studied many of the Talmudists and significant Jewish thinkers like Maimonides ("Teach thy tongue to say I do not know"), Rashi, and Spinoza, and a wide range of poets, including the great English poet Matthew Arnold, who established a cultural and philosophic division between the Hebraic and the Hellenistic. But I also wanted, as a young college student, to look to the Greeks — to Plato especially but also to Socrates, Aristotle, Zeno, Heraclitus, Epicurus, and Epictetus.

Arnold pointed out that Hebraism and Hellenism are polar opposites. He simplified the dichotomy between the two by observing that the former was tied to the moral impulse and the concept that sin and desire hindered right action, while the latter was all about the belief that intellectual impulse, beauty, and desire hindered right thinking. The Hebrews were about strictness of consciousness and conquest over the self, whereas the Greeks were about spontaneity of consciousness and seeing things as they really were. Could these be synthesized? Could Nietzsche's Apollonian and Dionysian? Could reason and emotion? East and West? Did duality need synthesis?

Whatever fragments I could press into service as part of an ethical code, I included as guideposts, though absolutes soon enough seemed unquestionably out of the question, simply because there were too many antipodes, too much dualism. My Jewish tradition had its split between the *Misnagdim*, or rational tradition, and the more mystical *chassidic* tradition, two utterly different ways of seeking and perceiving God. The Misnagdim were cerebral and analytic, while the Chassidim wanted to feel God in the viscera or, as the Yiddish would have it, the *kishkas*. The one tradition was much more bound up in study, and the other in miracles and vision. But both sought God.

I continued to wonder where God was and how I might apprehend him. Should I even be searching for a personal, concrete God rather than one who was mysterious, ineffable, and impenetrable? Despite seeing polarities in nearly every profound and philosophic or ethical question that presented itself to me, I embraced the notion that knowledge would lead me to wisdom, and wisdom would dictate rules of personal conduct and something tantamount to a belief system. However, a true belief system, I assumed, ought ideally to require — if even possible — a synthesis of ideas that would stand up through time. If I became learned and wise enough, I hoped, I might penetrate some of the metaphysical mysteries. That, I realized as a barely adult male, was probably asking too much,

considering that most people go to their deaths without knowing what lies behind the veil of perception, unless they guess
or leap to faith or suddenly find something ineffable stirring
in their blood.

Still, I was determined to enlist both heart and head,
Hebraism and Hellenism, East and West, and whatever else
might serve my quest. What spiritual pores I possessed would
remain open to the possibility of letting in supernal knowledge. I wanted to feel God, to ferret him out of wherever he
might be hidden. Or I would somehow ferret out the mystery, even slivers of it — I would achieve a greater sense of
what lies in the realm of spirit and nonmateriality. I preferred
the idea of having such knowledge arrive via my intellect, but
I was open to its arrival by means of mystical vision or the
miraculous.

In the meantime I could, as my Jewish heritage dictated,
do mitzvahs, good deeds, if for no other reason than because I
wanted to follow that ethos as part of my own evolving code.
I could ingest worthy ideas from the Greeks and the Jews and
all the major religions in forming my own personal Baha'i
without God. It would be a pastiche of different cultures and
philosophies, or what I began to think of as the Aldous Huxley
way, noting that Huxley cottoned strongly to the notion that
all religions had fragments worth weaving together into a full
fabric. And I could do that work with the hope that God might
be waiting to make his presence known to me, or that a spiritual epiphany might descend on me, or ascend from within. It
seemed to me that the question for any serious person of faith
was, where can one find God or the ontological source, the
spiritual design (if there is one)? If I couldn't find that, could I
at least discover a way to seek the source, one that made sense
and felt right?

It was clear to me that, just as there is a Hemingway existential code and an admirable American code of individualism and one of Emersonian self-reliance, there are valuable Jewish, Christian, and Islamic tenets and traditions, and we can set aside the best from each, elevating what each teaches, despite the centuries of killings and atrocities that have warped them. There was, in each, messages and homilies related to goodness, justice, charity, and love. All three major religions also spoke of forgiveness and salvation and the forging of higher mortal ideals. Could a person be undecided about embracing any single religion or singular notion of spirituality and still take the best of what religions offered and live an ethical and righteous life without God?

Many people, it appeared, did just that, and many accepted and honored the spirit if not the letter of the Ten Commandments without believing in the first three or taking a day off to make the Sabbath holy. At the end of the twentieth century, religious observance in America began to look more like a spiritual smorgasbord of interfaith practices and syncretism, and the numbers of those who did not believe in God or any specific religion grew significantly. More youth, especially, sought spiritual truth or practice without benefit of religion.

And what of the major religions of the East? How did they fit into my code? Buddhist wisdom, I soon learned, teaches compassion and mindfulness, that life is tied to suffering, and that one must move away from the illusory ego. I gleaned much from Hinduism, learning the value of good karmic acts even though I did not accept reincarnation, the basis for karmic belief. Religions taught love for one's fellow humans, a lofty and nearly impossible goal, but I thought I could at least try liking most people and seeking the best in them. I could eke out morsels of wisdom from the wide range of canonical teachings and doctrines even if I had to set them apart from God. And I had to set them apart from God because I saw God as missing in action.

The earliest code I learned of, aside from the one allegedly given by God to Moses, was the elaborate code of laws of the Babylonian king Hammurabi, which, like the Ten Commandments, was carved on stone (this one on an eight-foot-high monument). The code was tied to the power of the gods and promised punishment to those who defied it. Another code, that of the Roman emperor Justinian, was one of civil, codified Roman law that held sway over the Roman empire and included exclusionary rules, prohibitions, and punishments against Jews, pagans, and heretics. The Napoleonic code, made famous in the United States by Tennessee Williams's *A Streetcar Named Desire*, was a rule of law based on the Justinian code and French law.

The Laws of Manu, central to Hindu theology, spell out in the first chapter the Hindu cosmology and divine creation, followed by laws, duties, rules, and commands, which unfortunately fostered patent misogyny and the now-much-excoriated caste system. For thousands of years the Vinaya, or rules of conduct for Buddhist monastics, has been at the heart of Buddhist teachings, Buddhist ideation of spiritual ethics, and what the Western Buddhist scholar Robert Thurman describes as transcendent discipline. All these codes of law served many purposes, but for the most part they, like the Ten Commandments, spoke to established systems of belief and tradition and fostered order over chaos. Ancient laws are the result of ancient ignorance and prejudices, but also, like the Ten Commandments, of ancient religious and spiritual traditions.

There were also, of course, codes of human behavior embedded in many of the heretical doctrines that did not need to be linked to religion or to the isms they were based on, or linked to a God or rulers, but which provided useful and practical additions to my evolving personal code. These included secular humanism, John Stuart Mill's utilitarianism and pragmatism, and Marxism, with its emphasis on the collective good but without the ideological baggage and misapplications and pathologies that bred deadly policies like those of Stalin, Mao, and Pol Pot. And there were charitable ideals tied to the idea of the common good for the greatest number, to the ideal of living a life of service devoted to community, to doing the best for the most and in this way uplifting the oppressed working class, the lowly, the poor, the hungry, the forlorn, the sick, and those least able to provide for themselves. The enterprise of ferreting out my own personal code seemed at times a lot like what the Greeks would have called hubris, self-pride. But the search also struck me as necessary. Still, how vital was God or a higher order to any of these equations?

I learned from the great Greek philosopher Heraclitus that the only aspect of life that doesn't change is change itself, though later I was drawn to a remark of Tolstoy's that set everything off course once again by dividing it into elemental antipodes. Russia's great novelist said flatly that either everything changes or nothing changes. Keeping in mind the Socratic dictum to know myself, I wondered how much personal change in the course of a lifetime was possible. Sartre's idea that we define ourselves by the choices we make seemed to make the most sense. One can act with cowardice one day and courage the next. But is our fate our character or our character our fate? Nature and nurture presented even more dualism. In reality, I knew my code couldn't possibly be anything but a personal and pragmatic mélange of ideas that I would continue to extract from the wisdom of a wide range of sources, and that would, like time, remain in flux. But again, what about God?

I felt, as an American, that the encoded Declaration of Independence and the Bill of Rights gave me a nearly divine right to firm up an ethical code of my own, and that it would somehow be an individualistic American code. The Constitution told me I was endowed by my creator with inalienable rights. So what if I had doubts about my creator? So what if my code was a hodgepodge of ideas? I could still create and try to live by a fluctuating but meaningful and essential personal ethos. Couldn't I? Couldn't you?

Ideas cascaded through my mind that were linked to elevated ideals worth striving for — virtue and loyalty, generosity and selflessness, honorable and charitable and ennobling behavior. But I came to a roadblock when I thought, once again, of the words of Ivan Karamazov: "If God does not exist, anything is permissible." Could that be true? It seemed to be. What it meant to me was that any form of what we might deem morally damnable or odious was permissible in a world without God. One could do anything, be anything. There was no reason not to choose evil over good. In fact, as T. S. Eliot noted in writing about Charles Baudelaire, it is the choice between the two that makes us human, though it might, paradoxically, be better to do evil than to do nothing, since at least in doing evil we know we exist. This concept depends, of course, on believing in good and evil. But either way there was, in Ivan Karamazov's words, the reality of no enforcement, no power to intercede or interfere or judge in this world or any other.

I read the Marquis de Sade and was struck by his insistence on the pleasures of cruelty and torture without remorse or conscience or any necessary moral reckoning beyond enforcement of the laws of the land. Camus said, "There is no justice," and though he could have been talking about worldly justice, he meant an absence of justice in a world without God. In a world without God, men and women could, like Shakespeare's Iago, make evil their good, could adopt what Baudelaire and later Wallace Stevens called an aesthetic of evil. Why seek goodness or virtue or love or compassion or justice when evil, as Iago shows us, is much more vital and interesting, full of demonic energy?

Understand that I wasn't thinking of embracing black masses or devil worship or the likes of the satanist Anton LaVey. Sartre canonized the homosexual writer Jean Genet, calling him Saint Genet despite his having been a thief and a scoundrel, because Sartre believed Genet knew goodness better than one who had not trod the negative path. Genet, like Hester Prynne, transgressed, and Sartre was convinced this enabled Genet to better understand goodness. How did the idea of the negative path, of knowing evil in order to truly know good, fit into the calculus of a personal ethical code? And what was one to do about what Mark Twain so aptly characterized as the joy of evil? I was searching not just for answers but also for something that could give moral force to the choice of doing good, something that could stand in as an argument for the moral hegemony and moral power of God.

How could one know, without trial and error, if one is doing the wrong thing for the right reason or the right thing for the wrong reason? How could one assume moral wisdom in a world of shifting morality and an inscrutable God? How could one presume to create a viable ethical code without the certain deliverance from evil that an encoded law backed by God ensures? Morality and goodness, alas, are moored to time and place. How could one be assured of not acting in what

Sartre called bad faith, the idea that one acts for others or for institutions or, for that matter, for a code rather than for one's authentic self — if such a thing as an authentic self truly exists? The lyrics to John Lennon's "Imagine" continue to epitomize a utopian secular humanist view that sounds wonderful but has no force, no absolute, no imposed higher morality. It is a sweet and futile yearning for a sand castle in the sky made manifest on earth:

> Imagine there's no Heaven
> It's easy if you try
> No hell below us
> Above us only sky
> Imagine all the people
> Living for today
>
> Imagine there's no countries
> It isn't hard to do
> Nothing to kill or die for
> And no religion too
> Imagine all the people
> Living life in peace

Studs Terkel, the famed oral historian, once told me that he was an agnostic, and added that his definition of *agnostic* is a cowardly atheist. And Mort Sahl cleverly joked that when a family of agnostics moved into a certain neighborhood, a question mark was burned on their lawn. It's easy to be humorous about agnosticism. (Eric Idle, of Monty Python fame, told me the universe is full of two major forces — gravity and levity.) But if you, the reader of this text, cannot find God, if you doubt God, can you accept and obey the commandments that are supposed to have emanated from him? On what basis?

Must you accept any moral imperative linked to him or to the religions that exist in his name? If you truly accept the commandments without being able to accept God, if you remain without certainty, how then should the commandments or any religious moral imperatives apply? Can one truly operate according to one's own code, accept commandments or a personal ethos on faith without possessing faith and without a spiritual belief in command control? Of course.

I read Greg Epstein, Harvard's humanist chaplain, who argues in his book, *Good Without God*, that there are about a billion nonreligious people in the world who define themselves as nonreligious or secular, and that a significant number of these men and women are humanists who strive for a good life of virtuous deeds. Can one truly say, "I am agnostic about the first three or four or five commandments, but I accept or believe in a couple of the others; and I also believe that, even though God is not necessarily their author, the ones I choose to believe in I must obey"? Or should one, like the old joke about Unitarians, perhaps opt for calling them ten suggestions rather than ten commandments? The fact is, one can, and many do, truly take from what religions offer without believing in God, especially in this era of cafeteria-style approaches to religion and spirituality. Whether one can be selective about God's commandments and religious ideals apart from theist authority or theist certainty strikes me as a gnawing question answered inevitably by choice, though choice devoid of true certainty. Secular humanists may believe they are good without God, but they, too, must take it on faith.

Meursault in Camus' *The Stranger* is asked by a priest, as Meursault awaits execution for having murdered an Arab under the molten Algerian sun, what face Meursault has seen against the cell wall. Meursault had previously tried to see the face of Marie, the young woman to whom he feels attached, but had seen nothing. Too often we see nothing against the walls of our perceptions. To see nothing does not mean nihilism. Sartre built his entire edifice of existential belief out of being and nothingness. My longings continued to tell me, through the protracted years of my higher education, that there had to be more than nothingness, that transcendence was somewhere to be found, that a certain kind of numinousness had to be within my reach. I could find it, whatever it might be, while trying to live by my own code. Ephemeral flickerings would enter and dispel the void of nothingness and its accompanying dread. Must belief in God or in his absence carry static certainty?

Henry David Thoreau, Ralph Waldo Emerson, and Walt Whitman, after I first encountered them as a serious young reader, led me in what fleetingly felt like the direction to a higher plane, to the transcendent, to Thoreau's communion with the natural world, Emerson's Oversoul, Whitman's cosmic consciousness. Other authors, poets especially, made me desire union with something greater than my self. The great poetry of Ovid, Dante, Donne, Shakespeare, Blake, Keats, Dickinson, Eliot, Yeats, and Neruda hoisted me toward what felt like a higher plane. The bounty of the natural world and the birth of my children, too, would make me feel something that seemed to lift me upward. Music, which Nietzsche called pure form, and great art elevated what felt like my spirit. Intimacy and human closeness and love all did as well.

But different stimuli, different experiences, and the impact of random thoughts or passages of literature would change my perception that such elevated emotion was connected to God. Certain poets might elevate my spirit, but then I would let in the nothingness spoken of by the drove of nihilistic writers

and thinkers like Hemingway or Sartre, who made their in-
delible imprint on me and influenced my all-too-influenceable
young mind. Frederick Henry in Hemingway's *A Farewell to
Arms* wantonly kicks onto a blazing fire a log full of ants and
proclaims God a fascist. The old man in Hemingway's "A
Clean Well-Lighted Place" recites his nonprayer: "Our nada
who art in nada, nada be thy name." Sartre declares in *No Exit*
that hell is other people and dramatizes the seemingly end-
less torture and meaninglessness of human relations. These
would send me careening right up to the precipice of nothingness, and then a different text, a lyrical passage about love
or beauty or crocuses blooming, would change my mood and
shift my consciousness toward a higher plane.

  Even the profound notion of existential nothingness could
suddenly shift to a recognition of nirvana as an extinction
of consciousness, which in turn would lead to thoughts of
the infinite being comparable to the Zen idea of satori, and I
would quickly counsel myself that all I needed for a higher
and unifying consciousness was to remove the self, detach
it from ego and desire. But such a realization, coming under
no Bodhi Tree, neither stilled nor lifted my so-called spirits
any more than a stoic acceptance of nothingness. I wanted all
these musings to produce something spiritual, something that
could fill the void. I told myself there could be spirits, a host
of them, some *spiritus mundi* perhaps, beneath what we see
or know, undetectable like bacteria but affecting us in unseen
ways. "You've never been to Europe, but you know it's there,
don't you?" a Jesuit student once argued to me while I was in
college, after I expressed doubts about there being a heaven.

  I would abandon what suddenly felt like the foolish notion of an invisible *spiritus mundi*, and then once again feel
rushing up in me the demand for empirical proof of anything

beyond my senses or of a phenomenon not within the recognizable and quantifiáble material world. How foolish to long for spirit or soul or transcendence or static belief or a God one could actually know or see or feel or rely on, to want what the heart wants while the mind righteously demands proof. My feelings, I realized in college, were as capable of shifting from a longing for belief, to nothingness, and back again. I longed to feed my ego and yet to detach from the power it wielded over me. I despaired of finding God, even though I longed to feel him and to know him, to believe in God as the source of life and the purpose behind it and the one who bequeathed us the Ten Commandments, even though I knew they probably came down from a man who in all likelihood was called Moses.

Chapter 5

GOD'S IDENTITY

$\mathcal{H}$ ow do we see God or name or imagine him? The patriarchal figure has so long been with us, especially in the West, that the identity of God has become nearly inseparable from antiquity and holy writ. Freud suggests in *Moses and Monotheism* that the God of Moses could have been Aton, an Egyptian deity. Does it matter? Abraham's God was El Shaddai, the god of the mountain, probably derived from some pagan deity. Such holiness was attached to the name of Yahweh, the Hebrew God — such *mysterium tremendum*, as philosophers Rudolf Otto and Meister Eckhart called it — that ancient Hebrews believed the name was too powerful, too mysterious, even to be spoken. Jews came to refer to him as Ha Shem, which means literally "the name."

The holiness and mystery of God's identity served to make the creator and heavenly presence more and more remote from humankind. We can read the biblical passages about the one God who helped guide the Hebrews out of the wilderness and into the promised land, but what did the ancient people see when they saw their one and only God? What did they visualize? Before Adonai, there were graven images that the Hebrews could worship directly, like the golden calf they worshipped when Moses kept them waiting too long for the tablets. The golden calf was tangible. They could worship and adore it directly, could name and identify it and project awe onto it.

Adonai is a word used in awe, a substitute for *Yahweh*, and even *Adonai* is too holy to be spelled out in prayer books. Religious Jews will not say *Adonai* unless they do so in prayer, and men will utter it only when wearing a skullcap. Religious Jews write *G-d* rather than *God*. What extraordinary power the one God has. Even his name has to be concealed, just as he was concealed from Moses in the bulrushes and hidden behind fire in the burning bush. Was he plagiarized from the Egyptian God Aton, simply given another name the Hebrews made by transliterating the *t* sound to the *d* of *Adonai* — just as they took the ideas of hell and observation of the Sabbath from the Babylonian captivity? Freud even speculated that Moses was an Egyptian rather than a Hebrew raised by Egyptians.

How could the Israelites know the God of Moses when they weren't even certain what to call him or how to signify him? How could they apprehend him when he remained hidden, concealed in fire or shrouded with signifiers that could not be spoken even in prayer? Theological debates continue over the interpretation of scripture and whether Moses actually met God (Yahweh) face-to-face. Exodus and Deuteronomy appear to offer conflicting accounts on that score, but Robert Alter, an eminent biblical scholar, assures me that scripture indicates an evolution from the old traditions in which God becomes less visible as the Bible moves forward chronologically from the older tradition of Abraham in Genesis.

There appears to be little doubt in Genesis that Abraham sees God, in the great trees of Mamre near Hebron, where three visitors appear at his tent and a conversation ensues about the imminent destruction of Sodom. Two of the visitors turn out to be destroying angels, and the third is God, who overhears Abraham's wife, Sarah, thinking to herself and laughing at the thought that she could have a child. Robert Alter believes that, in the books of the Bible after Genesis, seeing God becomes taboo, and the often-translated idiom specifying that Moses sees God "face to face" does not mean he sees God's face, but rather that they have an intimate conversation. In fact, we are told in Exodus that Moses sees only God's backside. What part of his backside, I wonder irreverently?

Beyond knowing and imagining God, all one could do during centuries of anthropomorphic taboos was pray to a faceless God and importune, praise, and revere him without speaking his actual, unutterable name. Biblical translations made it impossible to know his name or know him conceptually, except according to what was taught or imagined. *Jesus Christ*, too, was not an actual name but a name bestowed by the Greeks on the alleged born-in-Bethlehem messiah. Yeshua ben Yosef, Yeshua son of Joseph, was his actual name, if he indeed existed. Today his name would be Josh Josephson.

Naming means signifying. Can we signify with a name something that is — like the name of God — what the deconstructionist philosopher Jacques Derrida aptly called a floating signifier? Or for that matter, can we believe with conviction in what Derrida, borrowing from James Joyce, called the presence of absence? Are the Old Testament God — Yahweh or Adonai or Ha Shem or Jehovah — and his New Testament son, Josh Josephson, who is worshipped as God, and Allah,

the Muslim God, all the same God who exists and reigns beyond our comprehension, beyond sight and name, in some
numinous haze of consciousness? (The comedic genius Mel
Brooks demystified the name Yahweh, the original name for
the one God, when he spoke of "Yahweh or the highway.")

For all practical purposes, God's name in our culture is
now simply God. But who or what do we see when we use that
all-purpose name? My mother would often exclaim in Yiddish:
"Gotteu!" (God!) or "Gott in himmel" (God in heaven). A
host of modern-language examples of common usage nearly
automatic to us, some with European roots, reveals to what
extent the power of God's name is habitually evoked. Many
still seem to think that taking the name of God in vain means
the actual name *God* or the name *Jesus Christ* — though both
are longtime pseudonyms. One often hears, as an exclama-
tion more than a question, "What in God's name?" or "In the
name of God!" But we also hear a myriad of other terms that
invoke God in common parlance. God forbid. God willing.
God awful. God rest his (or her) soul. Dear God! For God's
sake. Put the fear of God in me (or in you). God love you. Oh
my God! How, if at all, do such utterances of the name link
to what they signify, especially when many of us use God's
nomenclature automatically, without the slightest consciousness of who or what is being signified? Do we picture in our
mind's eye a presence conjoined to the word — some representation, anything beyond ineffable mystery or a white-
bearded patriarch?

It is still considered a sacrilege among Muslims to show the
face of Mohammed, Allah's prophet. In 1977, Black Muslims
in Washington, D.C., took 149 people hostage in an episode
that led to violence and death, brought on by false rumors
that Mohammed was played by Anthony Quinn in a movie

called *Mohammed: The Last Prophet*. In reality the filmmakers went to great lengths not to show any actor as Mohammed, or even actors as Mohammed's leading followers. Disney released an animated film about Mohammed, titled *The Prophet*, in 2002, after the 9-11 tragedy. Its filmmakers bowed to sharia by making certain no image of Mohammed was conveyed. Violence continues to erupt in the Islamic world over any representation, whether Danish cartoon or otherwise, of Islam's most blessed prophet. Martin Scorsese's 1988 film of Nikos Kazantzakis's novel *The Last Temptation of Christ* created an enormous stir (abetted no doubt by studio publicists for the sake of box office sales) because, as in D. H. Lawrence's novel *The Man Who Died*, Jesus Christ was portrayed as carnal. To be born of a virgin was to be separated from human origin and carnal genesis.

Throughout early monotheist history, humans seemed to prefer imagining the single-source deity — and, in Islam, the deity's chief prophet, Mohammed — as essentially inhuman and beyond human comprehension. The deity could not be represented in any way, could not be seen or was faceless, and was without a corporeal body or, in the case of the Christ and his holy mother, without sexuality. The miraculous was paradoxically, and perhaps understandably, often imagined as beyond human or what should be seen by humans, despite the natural human inclination to see and anthropomorphize, and despite scripture's notation that man was created in God's image.

Over time, a myriad of images of the monotheistic God of both Jews and Christians abounded, and God was pictured largely as a white-bearded, patriarchal figure, often on a throne, holding a scepter and with cherubim and seraphim hovering near. Voltaire put it best when he said God made man in his own image and man returned the compliment. The polytheistic deities, even the ancient Gods like the Mayan maize god and the gods and goddesses of Hinduism — Shiva, Krishna, and Kali — all had humanlike faces. Leonard Shlain wrote a way-out, original book positing that literacy reinforced the linear, masculine, left hemisphere of the brain and caused the disappearance of the goddess by replacing her with the hegemonic and androcentric masculine God of the Ten Commandments. We see him in Michelangelo's Sistine chapel fresco, creating man, and in the great Ghent Altarpiece painted by Jan Van Eyck in 1426 — though the beard of Van Eyck's God Almighty is dark. And in *The Creation of Man*, painted by the great Jewish artist Marc Chagall in 1957, Jehovah is an androcentric figure.

If there is a God, he or she or it could be anything beyond what we for centuries have imagined. Acknowledging this is no small matter. The famed eighteenth-century Anglican bishop and empirical philosopher George Berkeley, who wrote against agnosticism, made us acutely aware that a table is a table because of the fact that it is perceived as a table both visually and tactilely. How can we perceive God when we cannot prove God *is*, and we have only the representations created by others to foster or feed our perceptions? What refutes atheism is the simple fact that one cannot prove a negative. But if I want to prove God as a positive, affirm he exists in any form, I must believe or feel or imagine a presence of some kind that is beyond what is tactile and beyond sight and imagination or what language can signify. How does anyone do that with any certainty? Which is to ask — How do I, or any who seek answers we do not possess to questions of God's existence, create God?

Or are such musings merely the consequence of wanting a God who is concrete rather than an imperceptible spiritual essence, of wanting, perhaps, the God that the fiery American preacher Jonathan Edwards warned of when he preached about "sinners in the hands of an angry God"? Can we perceive God by an image apart from our senses and sense? An Internet image flies through thousands of miles of air to my computer screen, and I take the image's travels on faith.

Chapter 6

THE UNIVERSE AND
THE FACE OF GOD

In boyhood, I read with fascination and enthusiasm that the universe is infinite, and I read, too, many speculations about the likelihood of life elsewhere in the solar system or beyond. As an avid stamp collector at age seven, I was excited to see an ad in a comic book for stamps from Mars, Venus, Saturn, Jupiter, and Pluto. It seems to me now that the question of God and what he might look like is akin to the question of whether intelligent life exists elsewhere. Many might argue, as I do, that the mystery of God, like potential life in the outer reaches of stellar space, is for now beyond human comprehension. When the odd controversy about whether there was a face on Mars surfaced, I wondered if the debate was simply another attempt to find God's stamp somewhere beyond the earth, to see a face that was not earthbound. Does the immeasurable universe, the impossible-to-conceive universe — and the possibly infinite universes — represent what we call God?

We cannot truly see or imagine God, a concretized God, even though Hollywood once pictured the deity as the Jewish comedian George Burns. Hollywood also enlisted the black actor Morgan Freeman, a basso profundo, to play God on the silver screen. In the movie *Dogma*, we saw all rules broken in the casting of female rock singer Alanis Morissette as God. I've even noted an animated God with a white beard on the irreverent television cartoon show *Family Guy* interacting with Albert Einstein, who in his lifetime believed the cosmos was constructed too magnificently not to have had a guiding hand. That we ignore what once would have been a profound violation — of the taboo against giving God a face, let alone a human face, even a cartoon face — demonstrates, depending on your point of view, either how far we have come or how far we have descended. God can now have any face we devise for him.

The face of the one God, the God of the Ten Commandments, Jehovah or Elohim, remains as far beyond human imagination as the farthest of the galaxies or universes. We cannot imagine God or an ineffable spiritual order of our universe any more than we can see or know looking unaided at the night sky what is beyond the Milky Way. Maybe a vision in the desert or atop a mountain or in the holy city of Jerusalem can bring a flash of God's face to some, but alas, not to most. Orthodox Jews still cover their mirrors while mourning, out of custom and the superstition attached to the idea that an image of the forbidden face of God was not to be seen while praying. Mirrors were for vanity. Since man was made in God's image, a reflection of a face in a mirror was deemed to be a reflected image of God. One could not pray in the presence of such an image. Did man truly believe his face was like God's? Those who followed Christ initially, all of whom were Jews, must have been famished for a God they could put a face to. What we see in the story of Jesus, even though he had a nonhuman birth and was supposed to have risen from the dead in what can only be characterized as a distinct act of nonhuman posthumousness, is a God in human form suffering human pain and enduring a human death. This removes the Godhead from the nonhuman realm and provides, at least for the followers of Josh Josephson, a human face.

Did Moses see the face of God on Sinai? Did Jesus raise the dead or rise from death himself? Unanswerable questions are what make agnosticism understandable, perhaps even laudable. Many of life's enigmas remain. Metaphysical enigmas, if anything, appear to be unanswerable and, as a result, an understandable and powerful reason for agnostic thought. If we cannot see God or even fathom God's existence or know him except by faith, then why obey the commandments? Adherence to faith or existential choice would seem the obvious answer.

Perhaps all the wrestling with the very idea of God, as Jacob wrestled with the angel, and as I wrestled with establishing a personal code, is comparable to making things up as we go along, being pragmatic, waiting and seeing. My family often said, like a mantra, "We'll see," about nearly everything that needed to be decided, as if waiting for divine providence. That is why *Waiting for Godot* has always seemed to me an image of the human condition. We of little or no faith all wait to see, like Gogo and Didi. And all of us who live long enough to age are eventually struck with misfortune, like Pozzo, who is made blind, and his caninelike companion with the ironic name Lucky, who is struck dumb, by the time the play's second act begins. Where God is concerned, we without the anchor of faith all wait, and we are blind without the vision of a God who himself is mute.

Does God, as Einstein says, not play dice with the universe? Or as Stephen Hawking says, does God indeed play dice and sometimes throw the dice where they cannot be seen? Is God what Richard Dawkins calls the imaginary alpha male in the sky or simply, to quote John Lennon, "a concept by which we measure pain"? Or, as Christian doxology teaches its flock, is he the one from whom all blessings flow? And does all evil and suffering, all inspiration, all morality and goodness, also flow from him? I'm always struck when the winners of major sports victories or Grammys or Emmys start their speeches by thanking God. Thank first the first father who gave life to us all and him to whom all thanks are due. Father to us all. Original source of life. Giver of light. Bestower of blessings. If one goes back far enough in antiquity to the early cult of Yahweh, one learns that Yahweh was a merged God fashioned from other, mostly Canaanite, deities and had what may have been God's first and only consort, the goddess Asherah. God with a girlfriend! But it may be futile to attempt to prove who or what God is, let alone whether he ever dated.

The power of a play like *Waiting for Godot* is instructive, because one way of reading the play is to note that Vladimir and Estragon, its two main characters, are put on stage as we are on earth, without knowledge of where they came from or what they are supposed to do other than wait, which they do while being watched from beyond by those who sit in the theater's darkness. The strange and the inexplicable occur. Estragon is beaten for no apparent reason. Pozzo appears with Lucky on a leash. Pozzo is on the ground in need of help, and Vladimir surmises that this is a moment of truth, when he and Estragon are put on the spot to do something, to act, to represent all of mankind by helping another human being or, alternatively, by deciding to do nothing. The characters ultimately, of course, do nothing, because, in the most emblematic words of an entire play about nothingness, there is "nothing to be done."

We possess freedom to act and need not remain immobile when others are down or suffering. But we can also choose to do nothing. Establishing one's own code is a way of setting in stone — as much as is possible — how to act and whether to not act, choices one should or must make in life. Some like to describe themselves as apolitical, and in doing so they make a political choice, if they are indeed apolitical. "If you're unsure what to do," the Yiddish writer and Nobel laureate Isaac Bashevis Singer once advised me, "do nothing." Singer was pointing out the necessity of confidence in making major choices, as well as emphasizing that, if one chooses to act without certainty, such actions often lead to undesired consequences. Singer was a bit of a mystic and certainly a serious metaphysical seeker. He came from a learned, rabbinic family that was a marriage of different bloodlines — a *chassidic* father and a Misnagdim-raised mother. The central question of his work is the central question of much theological writing of all types: how much free will do we possess? I once asked Singer if he believed in free will, and he responded with the brilliant and paradoxical quip, "I have no choice."

Can one really say how he or she is bound to act in a dire situation that necessitates moral choice or has mortal consequences? It is far easier to call on a higher power, as if he were a lifeline like those in the television game show *Who Wants to Be a Millionaire*? People who believe that a sign from God can inform the serious choices they make in life, or that their choices are guided by God, have found a conduit that has eluded me. But why should my not finding God rule out the possibility that others have or might? I used to wonder whether I existed simply to entertain a presence who, like the audience for *Godot*, observed my actions and inactions from a place I could not envision. Perhaps I was being watched by an advanced life-form. Is God another form of science fiction?

As a kid, I read a comic-book science fiction tale about a time machine. The machine's inventor decided that the one creature on the planet that did not deserve to live was the mosquito. He hated mosquitoes and saw no purpose for their existence, so he set the time machine back to when the first mosquito spawned, went back, and crushed it. Then he returned to the present. What he found was a world without people, a world overrun by huge, primitive, dinosaur-like creatures. It was a simple allegory. Don't mess with God's plan, don't play God, or there could be dire consequences for all humankind.

God has moved out of the mythologies of the past into his principally masculine modern form, but why, I wonder, are God and time — notwithstanding the enshrining of the Goddess by many modern-day feminists and Wiccans — both fathers, while nature and the earth are mothers? (Gaia, the Greek goddess of the earth, is a maternal force.) Yin and yang. Patriarchy and matriarchy. Questions of gender identity connected to the spiritual or the metaphysical are profound and represent more antipodes, more dualism, perhaps more reason for agnosticism.

The homeland is often a mother. Soviets described the Soviet Union as the motherland, a term also used by Africans and anthropologists to denote the African continent, the site of human origins. One's land, notwithstanding the German fatherland, is matriarchal, as is nature. Like a mother, nature nurtures us and is identifiable with birth, so it makes sense that nature and the earth are linked to the figure of the mother. But if God is indeed masculine and a father figure manifest in the entire bounty of nature, why is nature feminine and a mother? Does nature as a mother work on her own, separate from God the patriarch, like Demeter, the goddess of the seasons, who in Greek mythology altered the seasons? In our culture, both time and death seem linked to masculine figures (however, one recent antitobacco television ad pictured the grim reaper taking off a hooded cloak to reveal an attractive young woman inside, who handed out cigarettes). The goddess Kali in Hindu mythology is linked to time, and those who weave our fates in Greek mythology are female.

But let us move from gods and goddesses and time and death back to the big question, the question of God. Is the question: what is God? Or is it: where or when is God? Perhaps it is more why? An agnostic who finds a moral compass can simply let go of the desire for an answer to why is God, and indefinitely postpone seeking an answer to what, where, and when, or can opt to dispense with them altogether. Many of those who seek spiritual sustenance are bootstrap agnostics disaffected by religion or unwilling to accept the built-in hypocrisy, contradictions, and demands of religion, with its bloody and awful history, its stringent moralities. Life becomes, as I noted earlier, a spiritual smorgasbord stocked by both the East and the West and not necessarily catered by God. Often the choices we make are based on an intuitive or emotional sense that there is higher meaning, and that ascendant or elevated feelings of spirituality are the trail to the grail.

Perhaps God, if he exists, is beyond seasonal change, beyond gender, beyond time, beyond space or matter, just as he is beyond our ken. Perhaps nature, too, is beyond time, and God is nature regardless of what gender we choose. Or is God time? The interrogatives are so many. Too many. God is love? God is genetics? God is evolution? God is randomness?

God is energy? God is molecular structure? God is salvation? God is transcendence? God is life? God is the ultimate moral scorekeeper? The fundamental question for the agnostic is simply whether God is. God is a hypothesis? I've witnessed gamblers throw dice at the craps table, hit their hoped-for number, and gleefully, gratefully shout, "There is a God!" I recall, too, an agnostic acquaintance of mine shouting out the same words with delight when a woman who had captivated him sent him an email expressing interest in dating him. Are such trivialities, which can feel like triumphs of the spirit, evidence of God? The thought seems, forgive me, sacrilegious. God is luck? God is getting a hot date?

As a veteran poker player, I have come to think of significant runs of winning hands as the result of streaks. Do streaks exist in poker or other forms of gambling? Do they exist in life? Good things seem to happen in succession, and so do bad. We often hear that instances of good or bad luck happen in threes, the number of the trinity. Is this simply random? In the fifties television show *Maverick*, the riverboat gambler and cowboy Brett Maverick advised others never to pull to an inside straight. Stanley Kowalski, in Tennessee Williams's *A Streetcar Named Desire*, brags about being lucky because he drew to one and got it. One takes risks in poker and in life and often does so with the feeling that there is either a winning or a losing force mysteriously lurking out there, often thought of as Lady Luck. I have drawn to inside straights, feeling certain I would pull the needed card, and have had exactly that occur. But I have also drawn to inside straights with the same strong premonitory feeling and failed to catch the expected card.

Most religious thought ties God to outcome, but outcome can be based as much on seeing God working outside the self in unseen ways as it can on seeing God prompting us from the inside. How often do we hear people say they success-fully played a hunch? This can be either ratiocinative or like the rapid leaps to judgment Malcolm Gladwell writes about in *Blink*. But is not a hunch often the belief that an interior reality corresponds to some external force, a feeling that a reality outside the self can be intuited? In the 1974 film *The Gambler*, loosely based on Dostoyevsky's *The Gambler*, Axel Freed is having a winning streak in blackjack. Holding a hand adding up to eighteen, he believes luck and his will can pro-duce a three card, so he doubles his bet and commands the dealer to "give me the three." The camera angle at the mo-ment Axel gets the three, a scene shot from below, makes him seem larger than life, majestic, Godlike.

Can we control life's streaks of good and bad luck? Can we intuit from some force outside us which way things are slated to go? Or is this force within us, as so many of the spiritually inclined reckon? Do we employ the power of our minds to af-fect cards dealt to us or to shape our destiny or human events? And to what extent do streaks of any kind teach us about the power beyond our ken that may or may not shape our desti-nies? This is the central question of the book of Job. Few have had a streak of ill fortune worse than that of poor Job.

Remember the craze over imaging? There were even bumper stickers enjoining us to imagine world peace. Charlie Garfield, a weight lifter and sports psychologist I knew, claimed to have discovered via imaging that he was capable of lifting far more than he ever conceived possible. Shakti Gawain sold millions of books about personal transformation through creative visualization. Channeling, too, became a pop-ular form of New Age spiritual expression, and there was sud-denly a host of New Agers channeling spiritual guides from centuries past. In August of 1987, the harmonic convergence

took place as those seeking divine transformation met together all over the world to hasten the beginning of a new
sacred epoch of divine love that would be brought on by a
conjoining of collective spirits, the triumph of a collective
spiritual will.

All these forms of human expression suggest a belief that
consciousness can transform the individual or humankind,
that it can establish magical or transcendent power or simply
hasten change. I remember thinking that, if creative visualization worked, I would have been another Michael Jordan on
the basketball court, despite my height, since I had from boyhood visualized myself making every impossible jump shot on
the court.

I often tell friends who are in distress that I will make sure
to think good thoughts for them. Not long ago, the children
of Lenny Shlain, a rational thinker and friend of mine who
was a surgeon and writer, and who suffered the scourge of
brain cancer, asked all his friends to think positive thoughts
on a certain day and to wish hard that the malignant, metastasizing tumor in his brain would disappear. He eventually
died, of course, but these wishful, heartfelt thoughts invested
with the power that is traditionally ceded to prayer may have,
some might argue, delayed his death a few weeks. How can
one know?

Can the mind really affect the world outside it? We never
did experience harmonic convergence, of course, but are we
so mind-body linked that cancers and their cures, as the Yale
surgeon Bernie Siegel has argued, are tied somehow to mind
and consciousness as is the world outside ourselves? Israeli
magician Uri Geller bent a spoon for me, seemingly with
his mind, in the radio studio where I interviewed him. I was
amazed to witness the feat, and though I knew I was being

deceived, I had no idea how he did it. Geller wanted me to believe I was seeing a demonstration of mind over matter; he wanted me to believe he had powers that went beyond mere spoon bending, that his thoughts and the power of his mind could, like Superman, actually bend steel. At that time he was advising investors in the search for valuable ores. It was perhaps important to him for promotional purposes to have others believe in him. He clearly wanted that from me. I also watched Kreskin the mentalist perform, as well as David Blaine and David Copperfield and other magicians who want us to believe they are defying natural phenomena and exhibiting supernatural powers.

Can we compel good luck to come to us in a cluster of fortunate happenings that seem beyond chance, that make it seem as if God himself is a magician, or we are? I hear a good number of neo-New-Agers talk about trusting the universe, as if trust somehow ensures the likelihood of an optimal destiny or an ongoing streak of good fortune. Would making luck occur by the power of the mind corroborate God's existence, even though many others have tried compelling luck with mind and prayer and failed? Is God the ultimate magician who fashions our streaks and shapes our destinies? Is there a link, knowable or unknowable, between consciousness and what lies outside it?

The linguist George Lakoff assures me that there are four categories of metaphors for God. Standard in Western thought is the personification of God as a father — the creator, judge, disciplinarian, shepherd, protector, nurturer. The one who loves us. Or doesn't. Then there is God as the infinite — all knowing, all powerful, all good, the first cause and the highest force, the infinite toward which or toward whom we aspire. This metaphor implies that we can get better, move upward. Less common and less popular is God as the source of all that is good in life. This is relevant to the Buddhist idea that the sun, stars, and sky all come to us. We are grateful. We did not earn these wonders, which in traditions other than Buddhism are seen as God. Then there is the God of the physical or fiscal world, our material world, which becomes sacred to us or of ultimate value. Most atheists, Lakoff believes, reject the first two notions of God but accept the other two. In that sense, most atheists, he argues, have a spiritual life tied to certain abstract notions of a God. God has to be understood metaphorically. Atheists like Hitchens, Dawkins, and Harris approach the unknown via rationality, but all of us use metaphor.

Here is an archetypal agnostic premise. God is unknowable and so, for the present, is the universe that humankind has long placed God in. Another is that each of us is a universe unto himself or herself, unknowable just as God and the universe are unknowable, despite our ability to observe and calculate and intuit and imagine much about each other. God and the universe or universes — be they multiple or parallel — are beyond our knowledge; but under this assumption, reality is approachable empirically and is determinate, or at least parts of it are, while, for the present, God and the vast expanses outside of ourselves that we call the universe or universes are not. We know no more in the absolute sense about our origins, prior to the big bang, as finite living creatures, or about our eventual denouement as a species, than we do about God and the universe or universes, though, as astrophysicist Neil deGrasse Tyson, the head of Hayden Planetarium and host of the television show *Nova*, vigorously insisted to me, what was prior to the big bang may simply be another yet-to-be-explored frontier.

A good deal of the past appears to be multivalent when

we recollect, analyze, and interpret — though there are obvious facts and much verifiability via data and consensus — whereas the future, or much of it, is beyond our consciousness, except for quotidian certainties like the sun rising or rational predictions and forecasts and guesses based on logic and past patterns or configurations and other forms of ratiocination. I remember a cartoon I saw as a kid in which signs pointed to the end of the universe, and when the fellow following the signs came to the end of the universe, he saw more signs informing him that this was truly the end of the universe, and that he must definitely stop. The signs assured it was no joke. This really and truly was the universe's end! Stephen Hawking wisely said of the universe's end: "The expansion of the universe spreads everything out, but gravity tries to pull it back together again. Our destiny depends on which force will win."

We do not and cannot know the universe's destiny. Though many interpreters of religious text assure us otherwise, such knowledge is beyond us. The universe may have begun with the big bang about fourteen billion years ago, but whether there was a Neoplatonic creative force behind it, a guiding hand, a cause behind the effect, or what the cosmologist John Leslie calls a fine-tuner, we do not know, may never know. When one reads someone like the paleontologist Stephen Jay Gould, it is hard to overlook the sheer chance and randomness of how evolution led us to where we presently are. Did the cosmos have similar chance-based origins that allowed the universe to come into existence, or was there a supernal force?

Modern-day spiritual believers do not necessarily see God on his throne, the cosmic joker God, the God Faulkner called the stage manager, a regal force deciding which wishes to grant or deny and meting out rewards and punishments, who handed his select list of commandments to a man who may or may not have resembled Charlton Heston. They do, however, tend to see our lives as having a higher purpose and themselves as destined for higher things. Yet here is the rub. We have no idea why we are here or how we came to be, except as the result of the fertilization of an egg that grew into a zygote from an initial coital act.

We are ultimately unknowable to ourselves and others. Our past and future are mostly unknowable. God is unknowable. For the present the universe — its origins and its destiny — is unknowable, as is whether there are many universes. Infinity is unknowable. These are some of the fundamental reasons why I call myself an agnostic.

Chapter 7

WHO ARE THE AGNOSTICS?

I continue to ask what was once the most heretical question of all — where is God? Zen masters teach that God is both everywhere and nowhere. Seek and ye shall find? No! Seek and find nothing! But finding nothing does not preclude the eventuality of finding something.

I have called myself an agnostic for many years now, ever since college, though admittedly with some fear and even a bit of trembling. *Agnostic*, like the name of God, is a floating signifier, a word with many meanings. There are men and women who call themselves agnostic but who don't agree with others what the term means. There are agnostics who eschew the label altogether, and still other agnostics who don't know that they are. There are theist agnostics, and atheist agnostics, and there are, in every one of the world's major religions, people who identify themselves as agnostics. And of course, there are the agnostics of the secular humanist variety.

There are probably more self-identifying agnostics than atheists, but in numbers, the former still likely represent only a small, though growing, percentage of the population in the United States and considerably higher numbers in western European nations. The many varieties of agnosticism, and the innumerable men and women who do not cotton to the name or remain closeted from it, make it difficult to quantify or categorize. Historically, *village atheist* was a nomenclature indicative of the marginal but conspicuous role atheists came to play in many scattered communities throughout the United States. We never heard the term *village agnostic*. Up until recently, being an atheist often meant persecution or scorn. The atheist proclaims with certainty, where the agnostic sides with uncertainty.

Agnosticism as a term began with the Darwinian T. H. Huxley, known widely as Darwin's bulldog, who introduced it into the lexicon in the mid-nineteenth century. Delighted with the fact that the term took hold, Huxley later explained that he coined it against those who seemed to have certainty about gnosis, who held on to solutions to what he saw as the insoluble problem of existence. *Agnosticism* is etymologically tied to the idea of being without knowledge — knowledge of God or of the realities of the afterlife or of any other metaphysical claims that Huxley saw as not revealed. *Gnosis* is Greek for "knowledge," and the knowledge that became associated with gnosis in religions both Western and Eastern was experiential knowledge, as opposed to intellectual or conceptual knowledge. Huxley's thinking was grounded in Darwinism and the reason-based skepticism of such thinkers as David Hume and Immanuel Kant.

To Darwin and Huxley, the subject of God was simply beyond humankind's intellect, even though Darwin fudged and probably feared coming entirely clean because of his devotion to his beloved pious wife. Agnosticism was for them, however, more about the lack of knowledge than it was about the lack of belief, though Huxley believed that both knowledge and belief were unattainable. Both Huxley and Darwin believed in reason, matter, and the forces of nature. Huxley proclaimed of God, the soul's immortality, and heavenly rewards and punishments: "Give me a scintilla of evidence and I am ready to jump at them."

Agnosticism as a signifier emerged from Huxley's wanting to stand apart from the idea of the Gnostic or divine knowledge, which, as I mentioned, etymologically links back to *gnosis*, the spiritual knowledge of the divine or the supernatural. This form of enlightenment emerges from intuition or revelation, from the divine spark within, from the heart. Saints were often used as examples of those who managed to attain gnosis, but many occult and esoteric and mystical thinkers have immersed themselves in a singular identification with gnosis integral to such traditions as the study of kabbalah — which has become a siren song to the singer Madonna and many other glamorous Hollywood types — and to the mystical teachings of the Rosicrucians.

Gnosis tied to Buddhism offers an escape from the delusional beliefs that are the source of human suffering. Gnosticism is a form of belief predating Christianity that came to be a virtual religion in its own right and is identified with various religious traditions, but it should not be confused with gnosis. The one who possessed gnosis was also believed to possess unusual power. Martyrs, mystics, and others who have experienced God on a deep personal level by means of gnosis are often seen as connected or linked to miracles. Can I, within my lifetime, discover gnosis, the miraculous, the imperceptible, the metaphysical? I consider it unlikely. But of course, my agnostic credo is "One never knows," and I don't.

When I was a high school senior, I took a course in international relations from Walter Kremm, the only PhD on the Heights High School faculty. I was excited to be in the class because most of the students in it were smart and ambitious. I remember Dr. Kremm impressing on us that events in the international realm could change dramatically and unpredictably with lightning speed. An assassination at Sarajevo and a blitzkrieg in Poland, and suddenly the world is at war. Later on, when both Kennedys and Martin Luther King Jr. and Malcolm X were murdered, and the maritime incidents in the Gulf of Tonkin were used to involve the United States in the ongoing war in Vietnam, I thought about how true the lesson from my high school teacher was. When I watched my television screen in horror as planes were directed into the Twin Towers and the Pentagon, the same thought crossed my consciousness, as it has during events that have unfolded in my own life that were unpredictably sudden and dramatic.

Consider the extraordinary changes that have occurred over the course of even a relatively brief stretch of time, and it is easy to understand how unpredictable human events truly are. What is true on the national and international macro levels is true on the personal micro level. A person of high visibility is arrested as a child molester or embezzler or murderer, or drops dead in the flush of youth, or is murdered, or is killed in a fiery automobile accident. A loved one is hit with a sudden stroke or a fatal cardiac arrest. Change is the constant. As long as we are in time's flux, we can count on it, despite what Tolstoy, who believed in the eternal, said, that nothing really changes. The spiritually anchored person, and the believer in deist providence, and the one who believes faith is part of a master blueprint drawn by an overseer all see change as part of ongoing purpose. To the atheist, change is simply change and randomly occurs as a result of no higher or invisible purpose, unless it is Darwinian natural selection. The agnostic, as I've said, takes a wait-and-see position, as Beckett's tramps do.

If there were a holy trinity of agnostics, it would be T. H. Huxley, Robert G. Ingersoll, and Bertrand Russell. A great orator, lawyer, and political figure, Ingersoll was known in his day as "the great agnostic." Ingersoll believed in the natural world and said matter-of-factly of the supernatural and the transcendent that he simply did not know. When I was a boy, my father used to tell me there was no shame in professing not to know, whatever the subject might be and however shameful it might feel to state one's ignorance. Knowledge, he wisely taught me, did not always come easily, at least not many kinds of knowledge — especially in that pre-search-engine world. In fact, not knowing and being open about it was, he made clear, a sign of humility, which was a virtue. My father was an autodidact, a learned man who believed that the more we humans knew, the more we had to realize how much we did not know, and on that, too, he was right.

It took much greater courage in the nineteenth century for figures like Huxley and Ingersoll to proclaim themselves free thinkers and to state categorically and publicly that, in matters of faith, they simply did not know. "When asked what is beyond the horizon of the known, we must say that we do not know," Ingersoll declaimed. And in his famous 1896 speech, "Why I Am Agnostic," he summed up his views when he stated: "He who cannot harmonize the cruelties of the Bible with the goodness of Jehovah, cannot harmonize the cruelties of Nature with the goodness and wisdom of a supposed Deity. He will find it impossible to account for pestilence and famine, for earthquakes and storms, for slavery, for the triumph of the strong over the weak, for the countless victories

of injustice. He will find it impossible to account for martyrs
— for the burning of the good, the noble, the loving, by the
ignorant, the malicious, and the infamous." Ingersoll could
not get past the traditional idea of a God who must be part
of the human experience, including all its catastrophes. Nor
could he intellectually allow theodicy, the vindication of God
for the world's evil, which I particularly associate with the
writings of G. W. Leibniz, who viewed God as having created
the best of all possible worlds even with the evil in it.

Many in the past century addressed or wrote about agnosticism, including Pope Benedict XVI. The then cardinal
Ratzinger claimed that agnosticism was indicative of the desire
for comfort. Since when do not knowing and uncertainty provide comfort? There is little comfort in not knowing and considerable more in knowing or believing one knows. Ingersoll,
one of America's finest orators, let audiences know with force
and fluency he did not know of what believers spoke.

I was hedging my bets where God was concerned as I
continued on into graduate studies. Perhaps I still am. Pascal's
wager, as it came to be called, was a form of guarded agnosticism named for the philosopher Blaise Pascal. I saw this
form of agnosticism in characters like my Uncle Joe, who accepted God and the commandments with the notion that, in
case there was a God and an afterlife, he would try to do the
right things and thereby find his posthumous reward. If there
was no God or heaven or hell, he had nothing to lose by doing right — though Joe was no moral paragon by anyone's
standards. He was greatly sympathetic toward civil rights and
concerned about black urban poverty, and he contributed
money to organizations like CORE, the NAACP, and the Urban
League. But he made his money with a pharmacy he owned in

the black neighborhood of Cleveland, where he sold, among other things, various assorted love and revenge potions, astrological readings, and horse-racing picks, and all kinds of other nonsense and gambling magnets. My father, no fan of his brother-in-law, claimed Joe watered down various over-the-counter medicines.

The problem for me with Pascal's wager was that, even early on, I couldn't accept heaven and hell. I was unsure about God and retained my skepticism with the hope of knowing him, of feeling him gain hold of me once again — though not exactly battering my heart, which is what the poet John Donne pleaded for from "the three person'd God," whom Donne wanted to "break, blow and burn" him. I simply wanted to have God in my heart. But at a certain point he simply was not there.

I longed for mystery, for ritual with meaning, for grace, for a soul I could believe in and for a God I could love and feel loved by, a God who could provide teeth to moral laws like the Ten Commandments and return them to my life. But since I had not experienced any of that feeling since boyhood, except when I prayed during the missile crisis, and could not substantiate God's existence, agnosticism, out of necessity, became my creed. All I had to do, my Christian friends would advise me, was accept Jesus Christ as my lord and savior and I could have all of what I longed for, as well as the prospect of eternal life. But my agnosticism remained obdurate, as immobile as the tree that, in the black spiritual, shall not be moved. Paradoxically, as agnosticism spread in my young man's veins and grew into part of whom and what I was becoming, and as I made the effort to concoct a code of my own, the desire for higher spiritual truth would pop up unpredictably in me.

Those who feel imbued with spirituality will say, omit God from the equation if you want. My response is to wonder how well those who speak this way understand their emotions. Bertrand Russell said, "We know too much and feel too little. At least we feel too little of those creative emotions from which a good life springs." The longing for spirituality is often connected to wanting more emotion, to longing for emotion to wash over thought and reason. Spiritual longing is also tied to the desire for higher knowledge or intellectual certainty, but it is the heart that wants God, and spiritual consciousness in general is wedded to emotion. Spiritual thinking is often not really thinking at all and exists apart from reason. In his excellent book *On Being Certain*, neuroscientist and novelist Robert Burton observes that certainty is experienced as thought. In reality, Burton argues, thoughts are sensations from involuntary brain mechanisms that function apart from reason. "I think it is so, therefore it is" is the fallacious thinking that anchors a great deal of faith and human intentionality to emotion.

To think or to feel there is a God or a higher spiritual meaning or purpose in one's life is never really to know or to confirm. This is what philosopher Jacob Needleman calls "intrinsic empiricism," and it doesn't hold water. Think of holy rollers and snake handlers and faith healers intoxicated with the fervor of what assuredly feels to them like the spirit of God. Think of talkers in tongues or fired-up preachers amid shouting congregants. They feel God. They feel the spirit of the Lord. What they feel, they feel; and the feelings feel real and launch thought and conviction and certainty, or are launched by them.

At AA meetings, alcoholics in the 12-step program rely on help from a higher power and have made famous the prayer by the Christian theologian Reinhold Niebuhr asking God to grant serenity. But a number of years ago, atheists and agnostics balked at that prayer and formed separate chapters, which removed the clause claiming dependency on a higher power. Agnosticism may sound like another kind of belief, but it isn't one I need to cling to or to keep in my heart or feel or cherish or rely on for greater purpose or meaning. Agnosticism is, in fact, utterly disposable if and when viable proof should come.

I can hear the true believer hectoring me: "When you need God, then you will surely call on him as you did when you went down on bended knee during the Cuban missile crisis. When you fear for your life or the lives of those you love, you will need God. When a disaster strikes or danger is imminent, you will call on the Lord. Or perhaps while you lie in irremediable pain, or as you gasp your last breaths of life, or as you look in wonder at a sunset as its final radiance plays on glistening water. You will need God, or you will fear God, or you will know God is there with you." Perhaps the true believer is right. I don't know. I only know that, for the present, I do not know God, and therefore I am an agnostic.

If God exists, what are his expectations? Why should he be responsive to our needs — why should he heal the sick or raise the dead or provide a winning lottery ticket? Does he truly want us to worship him and love our fellow man and woman as ourselves? What reason did he have for giving Moses the Ten Commandments, if in fact he did? What stake does God have in our complying with the commandments as opposed to our defying or simply ignoring them? Why should he care about how we humans behave and what we do or don't do, how we exercise our free will? Thinking of God having needs or expectations where we poor mortals are concerned is another

product of an anthropomorphic imagination, that in us which
insists on creating the creator. If he exists in some form or can
communicate with you or me, the creator nevertheless appears to be ultimately beyond human reason or imagination.
To know God is to feel God. I wish I could know him, feel his
presence, buy in, see the light, join the crowd. I cannot. I am
an agnostic.

What, really, does it mean to call oneself agnostic, other
than to be unwilling or unable to yield to belief and allow it
into one's bloodstream? Perhaps it is simply indecisiveness
or the inability to risk being certain? Uncertainty is often a
shield, but it can also be an intellectual necessity, an extension
of truth seeking. Spiritual hunger or awe or a flickering feeling of God because of desire or fear or the feelings of childhood cascading back can abruptly erupt and just as quickly be
vanquished by thought.

In the nineteenth century, agnosticism debates centered
on science and religion, and the natural and supernatural.
William James called agnosticism "the worst thing that ever
came out of the philosopher's workshop." In those days, what
agnostics had faith in, if one can call it faith, was the possibility of human knowledge. The Canadian novelist Margaret
Atwood told me her family of scientists had a long-standing
tradition of separating faith and knowledge, a tradition that
they saw going back generations. Both T. H. Huxley and Sir
Leslie Stephen, the father of Virginia Woolf and Vanessa Bell
and the man who published *An Agnostic's Apology* in 1893,
argued that we must suspend judgment when attempting to
understand the unknown, though both of these serious thinkers also expressed faith in the search for human knowledge.
Stephen rejected "dogmatic atheism" and resigned himself
to accepting limits to what we can know. Huxley refused to

assent to anything beyond the line of reason or the natural world without evidence, but kept his mind open to the possibility of evidence. Though some have disputed the idea that agnosticism offers a third way, since one must either believe or not believe, agnosticism has allowed for indeterminate neutrality between theism and atheism with an openness to evidence that might provide reason or explanation.

To call myself an agnostic is to claim part of a tradition that extends back a long way. Robert Flint, in his 1908 classic, *Agnosticism*, traces the origins of agnosticism to doubt- and skepticism-based philosophies in China and India, and to the philosophies of the Hebrews and Greeks in the Middle Ages, which eventuated in the seminal agnosticism that anticipated the modern varieties found in the philosophies of Kant and Hume. But agnosticism is ultimately a matter of individual consciousness and the individual's own will and disposition. Or, as Flint describes it: "Agnosticism is a learned ignorance based on self-knowledge and philosophical reflection." By its nature it is both highly personal and philosophical, and predicated on the unknowable and ever-expanding limits of human knowledge. When T. H. Huxley first defined agnosticism, he did so in terms of what he could not know, and appended to that his strong conviction that the metaphysical questions of existence were insoluble.

This was not ignorance. It was an understanding of the limits of the human mind, which continue to define what agnosticism is and ought to be. Huxley wanted to be convinced otherwise. In fact he couldn't have stated his attitude more clearly when he remarked, "To suffer fools gladly should be the rule of life of a true agnostic." I understand this to mean that one should remain tolerant and open to ideas of all stripes, and this is part of my personal code. It falls in line with the

agnostic ethos of never ending one's lifetime pursuit of truth
and knowledge even though they are protean and subject
to our flawed perceptions and mistaken judgments and our
search may ultimately garner none of the answers we seek.

In the sixties we heard that the personal is political. What a
good deal of my own reckoning with agnosticism comes down
to is that the personal is philosophical. Or is it the other way
around: is the philosophical personal? The relationship between
knowledge and belief is key. I cannot have the latter without the
former. Personal belief for an agnostic is not based on feeling
— as it typically is for almost all varieties of believers and spiritual seekers — but on knowledge. And for the agnostic, doubt
is the conduit through which knowledge passes and makes itself manifest. Socrates said, "Only a wise man can know that
we only know what we think we know and nothing more." He
is also credited as having said, "I know nothing except that I
know nothing." It seems to me these are useful premises from
which to begin one's search for truth or knowledge.

To Robert Ingersoll, agnosticism was personal. If you
read his most famous — and for its time, blasphemous —
essay, "Why I Am Agnostic," you realize that much of what
compelled him to establish his belief in agnosticism was a
harsh Christianity that he, beginning in boyhood, felt personally enslaved by — until he broke his shackles, his fear of
hell and eternal damnation, by declaring his agnosticism and
liberating his own deep uncertainty about the Christianity he
had been exposed to throughout his formative years and into
adulthood. To be able to say "I do not know" made him feel
free and grateful, and his essay is a celebration of his liberation from a religion that he goes after with a hacksaw of rhetorical invective and denunciation. Christ, to Ingersoll, was
just another in a long line of sun gods, a myth unworthy of

godlike status. Ingersoll, the son of a minister, goes so far as to state unequivocally that there is "nothing original in Christianity." He also takes on all religions by demonstrating that sacraments, symbols, and ceremonies have ancient origins, and that they duplicate ancient myths.

What I find most compelling about Ingersoll's essay is his narration of his personal knowledge-gathering quest and his assertion that knowledge is what set him free to repudiate the puritanical Christianity of his youth and to declare himself an agnostic. We find out how astronomy, geology, and biology all contributed to his break from the religion he found unforgivably severe in its demands for eternal punishment.

Of special interest to me is his mention of poets, beginning with Robert Burns and then Byron, Shelley, Keats, and Shakespeare, as singularly important figures. They opened his eyes to the iconoclastic nonbelief and uncertainty that were struggling in him to find expression. It was said of Ingersoll that, when asked what his Bible was, he would produce a volume of poems by Burns or the plays and sonnets of Shakespeare. In his essay he goes through a catalogue of important intellectual figures who opened his mind and left his consciousness irrevocably altered. Constantin Volney, Edward Gibbon, and Thomas Paine all get mentioned, as do Voltaire, Zeno, Epicurus, and Socrates—the last three, Ingersoll blasphemously remarks, are superior to Jehovah. It was precisely that sort of statement that prompted Ambrose Bierce, in his famous *Devil's Dictionary*, to link Ingersoll directly to the second commandment by writing, "No images nor idols make / for Robert Ingersoll to break."

Ingersoll also mentions the naturalists — Charles Darwin, Herbert Spencer, T. H. Huxley, and Ernst Haeckel — as playing an integral part in his acquisition of the knowledge that enabled him to pry himself loose from the darkling plane of Christianity and see the light of agnosticism. He propounds, as well, his theory of the indestructibility and infinite character of matter, which we now know to be incorrect. A grain of sand, Ingersoll argues, cannot be destroyed and cannot be created. It is eternal. Matter and force are inseparable, and both are eternal and cannot be destroyed. Nothing exists for Ingersoll outside of nature. What is especially interesting in this now-classic essay is not only Ingersoll's personal quest but the strong emphasis he places on the central importance of the pursuit of knowledge, which is really the pursuit of the infinite. We are likely fated not to get to anything approximating the infinite from a pursuit of knowledge, any more than we are to comprehend the nature or existence of the God of our fathers and mothers or the God we ourselves might invent or conceive or feel.

As with the first landmark agnostic essay, Ingersoll's "Why I Am Agnostic," the second was originally delivered as a speech, but it did not have the personal emotional stamp that Ingersoll's had. Bertrand Russell, mathematician, philosopher, pacifist, and Nobel laureate in literature, is without doubt the twentieth century's most famous agnostic. In "Why I Am Not a Christian," Russell argues that people are not moved by intellectual arguments but instead believe what they have been taught since infancy. The speech was presented in March 1927 in London under the auspices of the South London branch of the National Secular Society and later on was published as a pamphlet.

Russell was not the orator Ingersoll was, but while his words may not have raised the emotional temperature, or prompted believers to forswear their faith and enter the fold of agnostics, the speech is a model of intellectual rigor, logic, and clarity.

Russell begins with the assumption that Christianity is a vague signifier that represents, among others, people like himself who are Christian by dint of birthplace or geographic location. Christianity, Russell asserts, does not mean simply living a good or a decent life, and it is a religion that has become diluted since the time of figures like Saint Augustine and Saint Thomas Aquinas. Christianity, in Russell's analysis, comes down to God, immortality, and Christ. He concedes that Christ, who he suggests may not even have existed as a historic figure, offered a high degree of moral goodness, and that many of the maxims identified as having come from Christ are good.

But Russell, like Ingersoll, condemns the eternal suffering in Christian theological belief; he focuses on Christ's "vindictive fury" at those who would not listen to his preaching and alludes to Christ's cursing of the fig tree. Russell expresses his preference for Socrates and Buddha, saying that this was largely because they did not condemn to hell those who disagreed with them or were guilty of sin. Russell rejects the gospel-based notion of the Second Coming, but mainly, like Ingersoll (though without a personalized narrative of his own misery that had resulted from belief), Russell rejects the notion of punishment for sin as a necessity and calls the concept a doctrine of cruelty. He states that, the more profound and dogmatic the belief, the greater the cruelty, but he singles out Christianity — as it was then organized in its churches, and before the rise of today's varieties of religious terrorism — as "the principal enemy of moral progress in the world." Russell is especially critical of the Catholic Church and Catholic doctrine, citing as an example of the church's cruelty the wife of a syphilitic husband who must stay married to her husband because of the sacrament of marriage, and who, by church doctrine, is forbidden to use birth control.

The Catholic Church's argument for God's existence, Russell says, is arrived at "with unaided reason," and this, too, he sees as unacceptable. He asks the preeminent agnostic question — who made God? — and dismantles with reasoned counterpoint the arguments that base God's existence on first cause, natural law, or design, and the moral argument for God that Kant ultimately went to after all his counterarguments against belief in God. This is where Russell unflinchingly shows his willingness to shock, by suggesting, tongue in cheek, the possibility that the world may have been created by the devil when God wasn't looking. "There is a good deal to be said for that, and I am not concerned to refute it," says Russell. He then gives short shrift to the justice argument for God's existence by stating that there is too much injustice. God's omniscience he dismisses by noting that such omniscience, if it truly existed, would have been responsible for creating the Ku Klux Klan and fascism, as well as an earth that is decaying and dying.

Many of Russell's arguments have stood the test of time and have become part of what I oxymoronically call the nonbeliever creed. His refutation of Christianity turns out to be a strong, reasoned critique of religion in general and religious belief. He views both religion and religious belief as being about fear, which Russell calls "the parent of cruelty," and about the desire for safety, which, he says, "plays a profound part in influencing people's desire for a belief in God." He ultimately views religion as being accepted on emotional grounds and as advancing a morality that keeps human beings from happiness. He is unwilling or unable to see the consolations of religion. Russell's code is to look to science and reason and "see the world as it is and be not afraid of it....A good world," he argues, "needs knowledge, kindliness and courage....It needs a fearless outlook and a free intelligence."

In 1947 Russell delivered a speech titled "Am I an Atheist or an Agnostic?: A Plea for Tolerance in the Face of New Dogmas." In it he calls himself a rationalist and implies that his Christian education is the source of his rationalism. Catholicism once again is his target as he points out that the opposition of Catholic bishops to artificial insemination is "gravely sinful" and is based on biblical text rather than on rational thinking. Seven years before this speech, Russell's appointment to teach at City College of New York had been terminated. A court of law had found him "morally unfit" to teach at the college. He states that the decision was based on his position that the Bible should not be viewed as conclusive, and on his counsel that one should act differently from what the Bible prescribes — though there were also adulterous transgressions and multiple marriages in his personal life and the fact of his having been imprisoned in England as a war protestor.

Here, in this later speech, we again see Russell's clearheaded advocacy for the supremacy of reason and for conclusions based on science and probability rather than on faith and certainty. There are, Russell argues, degrees of certainty. For example, the certainty of Russell and the audience he was addressing the night of his speech is not the same as a British political party being certain of its position. Since there are also degrees of probability, utter skepticism is unacceptable to Russell, but he winds up concluding that what he calls the new dogmas are worse than old ones. Yet the heart of this speech is the question Russell poses in his title and asks rhetorically in the text. To a philosophical audience, his answer is that he is agnostic because there is no conclusive proof that there is not a God. In contrast, one could argue that the world is flat rather than round, says Russell, but probability deems the flat earth hypothesis likely to be wrong. On the other hand, to the man on the street, or for popular consumption, he would call himself an atheist, he says, because one cannot prove there are not Homeric gods, and, he concludes, the same holds true for Christian Gods.

Curiously enough, "the great agnostic" Ingersoll, too, somewhat muddied the waters separating atheists and agnostics when, in 1865, he spoke to a Philadelphia reporter, who asked if agnostics weren't superior to atheists in admitting their uncertainty, versus the atheist declarations of certainty. Ingersoll told the reporter that an atheist is an agnostic and an agnostic is an atheist. The agnostic, Ingersoll stated, says he does not know but does not believe there is a God, while the atheist says the same. In contrast, the orthodox Christian, Ingersoll argued, knows there is a God, but both agnostic and atheist know he does not know. The orthodox Christian simply believes. He cannot know. But the atheist, Ingersoll argued, is like the agnostic in that neither can know that God does not exist. My sense is that Ingersoll may have wanted strength in numbers via a kind of alliance of, or a consolidation in the thinking of, nonbelievers. In reality, many of today's atheists believe they do know that God does not exist and speak contemptuously about agnostics being too soft or wanting it both ways.

Sometimes I find myself thinking whimsically about how Russell or Ingersoll or Huxley might react to someone ensconced in today's world of spiritual thought — waiting for the universe to comply by providing a special, unexpected gift, or ready to receive a blessing from a source beyond reason or perception. Or how true believers would react to these three main agnostic thinkers, the true believers who cannot fathom how such thinking can flourish or even exist when they are devoutly aware of a God on their side whose presence they are assured of and whom they know to be just and merciful, beyond doubt or reproach. Even if suffering exists, the true believers would argue, it exists for a reason, and the Nobel laureate Bertrand Russell, in all his genius and rationality, cannot grasp the manifold and wondrous ways of God or the ineffable paths of a higher, though unfathomable, spiritual order.

Surely men like Russell and Ingersoll, as perceived by the religious believers of their time, damned themselves to eternal hellfire and suffering their blasphemies against Christ and Christianity. Or perhaps the believers imagined them suffering on their deathbeds, like the father in Evelyn Waugh's *Brideshead Revisited*, able to find in the last minutes an exculpatory act to hasten forgiveness as they obeyed God's demands and clearly saw the error of their ways and the light of Christ's all-forgiving spirit, in which they basked as they drew their last breaths — the divine glow of all-embracing love.

Chapter 8

THE FORCE THAT IS OR ISN'T, AND COINCIDENCES MINUS ANSWERS

*W*e might imagine how true believers would respond to agnostics or how agnostics might respond to true believers, but here is something I find hard to imagine. Please explain the following incident to me. I could say, before I relate it to you, "So help me God, what I am about to report is true," but my calling myself an agnostic and swearing to God obviously will hold no weight with believers. So just trust me when I say I am telling what my college roommate at Ohio University would have called "the God's truth." And here it is.

I had finished writing about the essay "Why I Am Not a Christian" by Bertrand Russell for this book when I took a break to read my review copy of *Indignation*, a new novel by Philip Roth, one of my favorite novelists, whom I was to interview a week later. Most of the story takes place at a small Ohio university that Roth calls Winesburg in tribute to Sherwood Anderson's classic work of fiction *Winesburg, Ohio*. The main character, Marcus, is in the office of the dean, a devout

Christian, and the two begin to square off. Marcus, a veteran high school debater and an atheist, cites Bertrand Russell's essay "Why I Am Not a Christian" and begins to recite from it lines he has memorized, and which I had just reread. What a strange coincidence! I am writing of Russell's essay one minute, and then I read the same lines in Roth's novel the next minute. Should these events be seen as conjoined in some mystical way, or was it a mere coincidence? I related the incident to Roth when I interviewed him, and his only response was: "What do you suppose it means?"

Of course I have no idea. If it were part of some unseen force, what would be the point? Randomness to the agnostic might appear to rule fate, though life can also seem marked by kismet, destiny, the Yiddish concept of *bashert*, or even what sometimes seem like karmic laws, the patterns and configurations that appear miraculous or beyond reasonable probability. If I'm dying of melanoma or my heart has nearly given up after a cardiac arrest, I'll hedge my bets and include in my treatment the allopathic path and nontraditional medical modalities and, yes, even the paranormal, another kind of Pascalian wager that does not require certainty. The agnostic waits to understand, because agnosticism is essentially a pragmatic credo of uncertainty about unproven and indeterminable answers. It is, as in the example of the Bertrand Russell–Philip Roth coincidence, more about questions without answers.

Many religious writers have felt inspired by higher sources, and, though the sources may be different, so have a host of poets, playwrights, and novelists. The act of distilling thought into words can simply be another wish for magic that might enhance whatever one is in the process of creating, making it seem as if it has greater sustenance and power. Wasn't that what drew Yeats and the others to Madame Blavatsky and the

Theosophists and automatic writing? The author Herbert Gold told me that Jack Kerouac, contrary to the myth he created about his writing, including most prominently *On the Road*, was not a one-draft, automatic writer. Novelist friends of mine like Amy Tan and Isabel Allende and someone I have known for years, the author Alice Walker — all, interestingly, women of color with strong religious backgrounds — appear to believe they are acting as mediums for the characters they create, writing as if directed by a force that takes them over. All three, not coincidentally, are spiritual seekers looking beyond the veil of normal perception to the paranormal world of unknown entities such as ghosts and spirits. Toni Morrison, the Nobel laureate and author of the famous ghost story *Beloved*, told me in an onstage interview that it often seemed to her as if her writing was directed by another source. It seems these authors are trying to find, or believe they have found, in their art a transcendent power that reaches them from beyond what any of us see, feel, or grasp.

I have long been struck by the way F. Scott Fitzgerald seemed to reach a level of the premonitory in *The Great Gatsby* that he probably had no idea he was traversing. Think of the prototypical fascist Tom Buchanan in the novel, or the Jewish gangster figure Meyer Wolfsheim, with his human-molar cuff links and his ownership of the oddly named Swastika Holding Company, as well as Fitzgerald's use of the word *holocaust* toward the novel's end, and you get a sense of what I mean. Those elements, written in 1925, suggest to me a weird and inexplicable tapping into the future. Or perhaps they don't. Blake quickly comes to mind as a poet who exhibited a seer-like power in his art, and many would argue that art can provide access to a higher or greater, inexplicable source as it deploys us into a different state of consciousness. Many artists embrace, of course, the popular belief that art provides a substitute for religion or religious belief.

Mark Twain used to contend that if one hadn't heard from someone in a long time and wanted to hear from that person, all he or she had to do was type a letter to the person and, without sending it, would hear back. The premise seems doubtful to this doubter, but Twain swore by it. The Chilean novelist Isabel Allende swears that a Hail Mary will always get her a taxicab. Dan Langton, a longtime academic colleague of mine and one of the lesser-known poets of the Beat movement, told me the story of his wife, Eve, who is Jewish, going to the holocaust museum in Washington, D.C., where every visitor, upon entering, receives a card randomly chosen from thousands of cards, each bearing the name and photo of a victim of the holocaust. Eve was born in Berlin as Eva Heymann, and she was given a card with the photo of a young woman who had the same name, Eva Heymann, as well as her identical date of birth. Thousands of cards to pick from, and Eve, who was emotionally torn up by the weirdness of the experience, somehow was given this one.

How does one explain such a bizarre coincidence? One cannot. It could simply be a freakish example of randomness and nothing more, but it provokes one to search in all directions for answers and to muse along lines that are irrational, nonempirical, unverifiable. Is there a source for such odd and inexplicable events? Perhaps there is, but of course, perhaps there is not. Many believers and spiritual seekers hope or insist there is. "Everything happens for a reason" is the puerile-sounding cliché that sums up the wish for a source that makes events explicable that otherwise are not, that leads to the belief that loss and tragedy and failure are all part of some master teacher's lesson plan orchestrated by a force that guides us, thus ensuring reason. It is belief in a divine form of engineering.

Most often, though perhaps less so in recent years, that force has been identified with God, the higher power, the ultimate author of our destinies and of the Ten Commandments. According to this line of thinking, life teaches us lessons, and they are devised by an omnipotent moral pedagogue or some other unnamable force or spirit beyond our ken. It is enviable that some people believe such a force is operating and are certain it will ultimately reap for them what is right or good or true. Even skeptics and agnostics may sometimes wonder if inscrutable events, eerie coincidences, synchronicities (the term Jung fancied), and life's bizarre serendipities are all determined solely by randomness.

An inexplicable coincidence occurred after I wrote a story based on a young woman who thought she was in love with me and stalked me when we were both in college. I had foolishly had sex with her but was uninterested in pursuing anything after that. The sex had been consensual, and I hadn't led her on, but she would suddenly appear outside of classes I was taking or turn up at the trailer I rented in the woods during what I liked to call my Thoreau phase. She would call me "just to talk" and send notes, which began to take on a begging quality as she told me she just had to see me. I found her actions increasingly annoying and came to realize that she was disturbed and obsessive, but I tried to maintain my code of courtesy and kindness. Anyone who has experienced the feeling of being pursued by an especially needy, unwanted suitor knows it is most unpleasant.

I followed my code until she showed up at my home in Cleveland during a spring break while I was off with friends, asking my mother if she could see me and being so insistent that it actually frightened my mother. That, of course, angered me. It turned out that a friend of mine, who was working toward his PhD in psychology and doing clinical work with patients who were undergraduates, called and told me, against all the rules, that she was his patient and I should cut her loose, that my being kind and not rejecting her was only feeding her false hopes. I followed his advice and refused to engage with her. The next thing I knew, I heard from a minister who told me he was with her in the emergency room of the local hospital. "She took all kinds of pills and nearly died," he informed me, and then added abruptly: "It's because of you. You need to come see her." I was conscience stricken and didn't know what to do. I called my psychologist friend, who told me, in a voice filled with certainty: "It's emotional blackmail. That's all it is. She really doesn't want to kill herself. She needs to be rejected. Stop being the nice guy. She needs to see you as an asshole. Don't see her. In fact, the best thing you can do is tell her to fuck off."

This represented a serious moral quandary for me. My code urged me to be a good guy and see her and try to offer comfort to her troubled soul, even though her behavior had been way over the top. My friend, her therapist, was extremely intelligent, and I assumed he must know the right action for me to take — or in this case, the correct nonaction to take. So I settled on not seeing her, despite my fear that I was making the wrong choice, violating my code. I thought, "What if she does kill herself? Would that be on me for the rest of my life?" I wanted to set things right. What if my psychologist friend was wrong?

The point of this story is not only the moral quandary I faced in trying to follow a code that shifted around and made following it impossible. It was clearly a judgment call for me, but it was also clear that she was using the attempted suicide and the minister and her hospitalization as a way to force me to do something I did not want to do. I did not want to be responsible for this young woman's fragile mental state, which conceivably could have led to another, successful suicide attempt. And I believed my psychologist friend was probably right. Ultimately, I did not want to see her, and chose not to. She, fortunately, did not kill herself, and the stalking stopped.

But there is a bizarre denouement to this story. These events all occurred in 1965, the year I decided to reside in the trailer in the woods. Over a dozen years later, when I wrote a story based on the encounters I had had with this young woman and on her attempted suicide, I mailed the story to a small literary quarterly, depositing it in the outgoing mail slot in the mail room of the university's School of Humanities, where I was teaching. Immediately afterward I checked my mailbox for incoming mail. In it was a postcard from her.

The skeptic in me always thought this was pure coincidence — her writing me out of the blue after more than twelve years, telling me that she lived in New Jersey, where she was a professor, saying that she was headed to San Francisco for a meeting, and asking if I would meet with her. I thought enough time had passed, and, still wanting to follow the code of kindness and civility, and perhaps out of a perverse curiosity as well, I agreed — though I never heard from her again. It was as if she had merely wanted an acknowledgment that I would see her. But when I saw her postcard in my mailbox immediately after mailing the story about her, the hairs on my arms stood at attention. Was it like when you write a letter to someone and, as Twain suggested, you don't mail it? As if some kind of magic were at play, or as if you had somehow conjured the person? I found myself responding with a skeptic's

Melvillean "No," but there were, I knew, plenty of quirky stories, many of them far more dramatic, and some right out of
Ripley's *Believe It or Not*.

I recall a story about a man in Mentor, Ohio, which is near
Cleveland, where I grew up. The man's young son went swimming in a lake one day and disappeared, presumably drowned.
The family wanted the boy's body, and there were intense
searches for it. Everything possible was done over the following weeks to recover the body, but without success, and the de-
spairing father decided it was important for his peace of mind
to take his boat out on the lake and fish. Once out there, he
snagged what turned out to be his son's body. I recall reading
the story and wondering if it was made up or a kind of cosmic
joke. My agnosticism labeled it one of life's bizarre, random
coincidences, an inexplicable riddle of existence. But I could
see how it was a Rorschach test for believers and nonbelievers.
Perhaps it meant something, but then, perhaps it did not.

I suspect the need to believe in explanations that link inexplicable events to a higher force has to do simply with the
wish for such a force to exist. One can see the appeal of a television series like *The X-Files*, which seems to tell us there is
something out there, rather than nothing, even though that
something operates beyond what the human mind can comprehend. It is mysterious and spooky to me that Eve Heymann
Langton would get a card remembering a Shoah victim who
had the same name and birth date as hers, or that I would get a
postcard immediately after mailing the story I'd written about
the young woman who had stalked me more than a dozen
years earlier, or that the Ohio father would snag his son. But
what do such examples reveal?

The great Yiddish writer Isaac Bashevis Singer, who spent
his adult life fascinated by the paranormal, wrote a story,

"Fire," about a man, Leibus, who was tormented with envy of and rage against his remarkably fortunate and successful brother, Lippe. Lippe was their father's favorite son, while the narrator, Leibus, was despised by his father, who had habitually beaten him and left him nothing in his will, even though Leibus had provided all the necessary care for his father during his final, invalid years. The inheritance was left to Lippe, who had married a beautiful woman and had lovely children, and who, despite or because of his unscrupulousness, had become fabulously wealthy, while Leibus had no bride or progeny and barely survived as a pauper.

Possessed by envy, Leibus hatched a plan to burn down his brother's home, granary, and mill, and he trudged out to do so with a bag of shavings, two flints, and a wick. Just as he was about to do this terrible deed — feeling as if he were impelled by an outside force, by some dybbuk that had managed somehow to enter him — he came to his brother's home and mill and saw that both were on fire. He tells us in the tale: "I had come to set a building on fire and it was already burning." What a strange coincidence! He screams for help, and the peasants who hear him come and put the fire out, but not before Leibus heroically races in and rescues his brother and his brother's family from what would have been certain death. Since he was there and everyone knew of his enmity for his brother, he was assumed to be the perpetrator.

In telling his long-kept secret from inside the poorhouse and relating the strange coincidence, he approaches death wondering if it was his anger that started the fire. He asks the reader, "What do you think?" I ask the same question: What do you think of the improbable occurrences in life that seem too eerie to be accidental? Are they just chance, or is there a force, perhaps beyond our understanding, that produces these events? To what purpose or to what end? Can anger create a blaze?

As I have repeatedly said, I am a doubter, and I doubt that thought can act as a catalyst to events such as the one we see in the Singer story, or that it influences synchronicity, as Carl Jung defined it — "the meaningful coincidences" that occur without rational explanation, without any visible connection between cause and effect. The often-cited, classic example is Jung's patient who related a dream to Jung about a scarab, when a flying beetle suddenly appeared in the room. One can explain such coincidences as simply coincidences and nothing more, but Jung believed a mystical or transcendent element was at work. The inner life of the individual and his or her mythical unconscious were somehow connected to the external world of phenomena, according to Jung, and he saw this sort of connection as a plus for the divining therapist. Of course Jung also believed in spiritualism, astrology, telekinesis, and a lot of Nordic hocus-pocus. One would be hard pressed to describe him as a rational thinker, even though he started out as an acolyte of Sigmund Freud, the great Victorian thinker who felt bound to rational thought.

Generally, skeptics view synchronicity as similar to other paranormal phenomena. All such phenomena, most skeptics say, can be explained either by means of rational empirical evidence or simply by probability or chance, regardless of how extraordinary or random they may seem. Psychics who predict the future or ferret out the past in ways that seem to defy rationality are either up to tricks or simply lucky enough to get hits. Skeptics will quickly tell you that the misses far outnumber the hits, but when there are dramatic or inexplicable hits, the hits rather than the misses are what people remember. And yes, there are anecdotal stories of hits that defy

probability and chance, that seem uncanny and beyond reason. Agnostics remain skeptical. Belief in a controlling nature
behind synchronicity, like belief in psychic readings, premoni-
tions, and most spiritual and mystical forces, rests on the idea
of a link to a power beyond our rational faculties. For psychic
phenomena truly to exist, there must be a link between the individual consciousness and the unseen world outside of what
is rational.

A funny and revealing story comes to mind. I had an
accountant named Bob Steiner who was also a magician — I
liked saying my accountant was a magician. Steiner became
rather well known in the world of skeptics and debunkers,
and appeared many times on television and radio as a bogus
psychic. In fact he worked with the famous magician James
Randi; he and Randi exposed a phony faith healer named
Peter Popoff, who used an electronic device that fed him information through an earpiece. Popoff's wife would tell him,
through the earpiece, people's ailments as he approached
them in the audience, and he would amaze everyone by noting, supposedly with help from God, what they were suffering from or where they were in pain or what they had been
diagnosed as having — all information acquired ahead of
time by Mrs. Popoff.

Steiner happened to mention to me that he was doing a
television show for the Fox network based on the life of Harry
Houdini. He informed me that they were going to do a séance
in which they would attempt to get Houdini to speak from
the dead, because Houdini had debunked many séances and
swore he would communicate from the afterlife if one existed. It all sounded like good entertainment to me, and when
I asked Steiner who was producing the show, he told me it was
a fellow named Ken Ehrlich.

Now Ken Ehrlich had at one time lived three houses away from me in Cleveland, and we had belonged to the same college fraternity. My sister had been his babysitter when he was a child, and our parents were friends. He had gone on to produce the Emmys and the Grammys. Ehrlich had no way of knowing I knew Steiner. Steiner had impersonated a psychic on many occasions, all over the world, as part of his debunking crusade, and he was good at it. When set against others who claimed they were real psychics, he inevitably got audiences to believe in the superiority of his psychic powers. Then he would reveal that he was a skeptic and a magician impersonating a psychic. I asked him when he was planning to see Ehrlich, and he told me they had a meeting set up for a week later, in Beverly Hills. I proceeded to reveal to him many facts about Ehrlich that few people, except those from Ehrlich's past, could know.

When Steiner met with Ehrlich and Ehrlich's assistant producer, Steiner went almost immediately into his psychic role, insisting right off to two skeptical men that he possessed paranormal powers. To the assistant producer, he made general observations of the sort that anyone might buy into, and then he told Ehrlich that he had never before felt such powerful psychic vibrations as he felt with Ehrlich. He started off by saying he saw a diamond and a couple of older people. Did that have any significance? I had told Steiner that Ehrlich's grandparents' name was Diamond. I had also heard from my mother a few months earlier that she and my father, who were still friendly with Ehrlich's parents, had attended the bar mitzvah of his brother Steve's son in Cleveland. Steiner asked Ehrlich if he had a brother, and when Ehrlich said he did, Steiner asked if there was a recent celebration or ritual having to do with the brother's son.

All this was pretty surprising to Ehrlich, but he deduced that Steiner must have talked to his wife. "You spoke to my wife, didn't you?" Ehrlich asked. Steiner looked Ehrlich right in the eye and sternly said, "I swear on everything, including my own life and the lives of my children, that I have never met or talked to your wife." Whereupon he asked Ehrlich another question gleaned from my supply of information: had he dated a girl in college with a peg leg? Ehrlich became, according to Steiner's description, highly agitated, exclaiming that his wife didn't know about this girl, who unfortunately had come to be called Peg Leg Betty. Steiner told me he felt compelled at this point to let Ehrlich know the truth because Ehrlich was begging. Steiner blurted out, "Mike Krasny says hello."

It's hard to say how long Steiner might have been able to play out the charade, but the point is that he had a source that the others, Ehrlich and his assistant producer, did not know about and could not see or imagine. If events occur in our lives that seem extraordinary or magical, there are often rational reasons behind them that can be uncovered with more information. Skeptics strongly believe this is the case with UFOs and other paranormal phenomena. A group of Bay Area skeptics, which Steiner used to head, have offered a significant cash reward to anyone who can prove, under their controlled conditions, a paranormal phenomenon. To date, no one has claimed the cash. I think the sort of display it would take to satisfy this challenge is analogous to what agnostics would like to see or experience that would convince us that a supreme being or higher consciousness exists.

I know a woman who consulted a psychic after the death of her father. She was inconsolable until the psychic informed her of certain facts about her father that the grieving woman claimed no one outside her immediate family could possibly have known. Were there information sources she was unaware of, or was the psychic simply lucky to make hits out of the blue? Or what of the other alternative — the power of the mind to pull in information that would otherwise be inaccessible or that comes, via some preternatural ability, from sources beyond normal perception? Those who claim they possess psychic powers, like the former ballroom dance instructor John Edward, who claims to talk to the dead, usually avow that such psychic or spiritual abilities are accessible to every one of us. Bob Steiner and other skeptics would dismiss such phenomena out of hand and would do the same to all those stories we read, especially in the tabloids, or see dramatized on TV, about psychics helping police locate a lost or kidnapped child or a murdered corpse.

I'm not sure I would dismiss all such stories out of hand, just as I am not ready to dismiss God out of hand or the idea that prayer might help. How can such matters be proven or disproven? I interviewed Larry Dossey years ago, a physician who insisted that he had proven, with double-blind experiments, the efficacy of directed prayer at a distance, the idea that one can alter the health of another through prayer, even someone who is entirely unknown to the one who is doing the praying. Though Dossey's experiments have been debunked, how can we prove or disprove absolutely, especially in every instance, that such claims or miracle cures — not to mention near-death and out-of-body experiences and other examples of what to some is paranormal reality — are just pseudoscience or utter nonsense?

How can we determine if dreams can reveal another dimension, or if they possess premonitory power, that they are not simply what Freud called the royal road to the unconscious, or what Harvard's Allan Hobson posits is the flotsam and jetsam of everyday neurophysiologic fragments? How can we know whether what seems to be good or bad luck is the result of pure chance or tied to a source without, within, or both? Is it better to be certain and wrong or simply uncertain? I have no answers, and I envy those who do, because certainty, even if it proves unremittingly wrong, can bring respite from the most distressing pain and despair.

Much of the paranormal elicits analogies to agnosticism. Studies at Duke University in the 1930s — led initially by J. B. Rhine, who coined the term *ESP* — used Zener cards, which have clearly marked symbols on them, in an attempt to locate individuals with the power of clairvoyance. The study never succeeded in proving the existence of extrasensory perception, or for that matter telepathy. ESP, like many spiritual feelings or belief in hunches and precognition and prescience and synchronicity and other intuitive or paranormal phenomena, is often rooted in what people feel to be real because of anecdotes from their lives or the lives of others that, in their minds, support certainty. There is a vast number of stories about people predicting the future through an intuitive feeling or a dream, people who, in these instances, were warned of something that otherwise would never have consciously occurred to them. Or someone appears in a dream who has not been thought of in decades, and that person suddenly phones or appears soon afterward during waking hours. An intuitive feeling of good tidings abruptly washes over a person who then discovers an unanticipated or unexpected joy or stroke of good fortune. A foreboding feeling comes, and it turns out to presage some dark episode or painful event.

What such occurrences prove or disprove is ultimately moot and for the most part dependent on individual perceptions, which depend on feelings. My Aunt Pearl was a superstitious woman, and when I dropped a butter knife one day, she told me it meant for certain a letter would arrive for me in the day's post. I was eleven years old and almost never received mail, but that afternoon a chain letter came addressed to me from a school chum. And there was a tale in my mother's family history that no children should be given first names beginning with the letter Z or they would die, because that is precisely what happened to three children in the family, born to three different sisters of my mother. The three sisters had all wanted to name their children after their maternal grandfather, Zalman. My mother concluded that Zalman wanted the children's souls, and that was why they had died. This did not seem to be a reasoned explanation, but when I was discussing possible names for my children, there was no way I would have opted for a name beginning with the letter Z.

When I was in my thirties, I dreamt that my black Labrador retriever, Nemo, who had been perfectly healthy the evening before I went to bed, died. That next morning, immediately following the dream, Nemo appeared ill to me, and I took him to the veterinarian and discovered he was experiencing renal failure. How many stories do we hear of unlikely events of this sort? What, if anything, are we to make of them? Are they all simply the result of chance? The agnostic mind seeks answers, but the available answers all too often lead to the inexplicable and more questions.

Chapter 9

FROM NOWHERE TO SOMEWHERE
Spiritual Envy

Like most literary scholars and literature teachers of my era, I had come, as a young professor of literature, to greatly admire the poet T. S. Eliot, despite his cold, Tory Anglicanism and anti-Semitism. Could one truly be, I wondered, in what Eliot called the now that is always now? All our nows seem to fall into time's relentless flux. God, and only God, can be eternal, while life remains ephemeral. That is perhaps why Moses needed God to back up the commandments.

What was there to believe in when all was impermanent? Evanescence and nothingness began to go together in my mind, like "love and marriage" and "a horse and carriage" in the old song. I often felt as if nothingness was the very core of existence. How could life mean anything in the face of death? Belief in nothingness — often existentially connected to the inevitability of death — made a personal code, like everything else, seem absurd. So many of the contemporary writers and philosophers I studied and was influenced by seemed to

have come around to a belief in nothingness, though, paradoxically, they nevertheless were compelled to create, and
many, like Beckett, who joined the underground fight against
the Nazis in World War II, were politically active.

Belief in nothingness could be terrifying, but it could
also protect me from my inability to find spiritual answers
or a higher spiritual purpose. I would apply, just as children
often do, the simple question of why to a host of assertions of
meaning, and the whys would lead to nothingness. You want
to be a doctor? Why? Because you want to heal and help humanity like Albert Schweitzer? Why? Because you think it's
ennobling and high-minded and rewarding? Why? Because
you believe in goodness and humane ideals? Why? On and
on and on. Like the badgering questions of a child, this line of
inquiry can go on to infinity. It turns out, from the perspective
of a belief in nothingness, that the road traveled, any road,
goes nowhere except to the road's end, and the roads themselves mean nothing. Any meaning we hope to eke out of life,
even if we feel such meaning is worthy, is illusory. Posterity
and ongoing generations? Love and valor and decency and
humanity, goodness and service and noble callings? None of it
means anything, because nothing can mean anything.

Nothingness is a splendid pose. Nothingness invades one's
consciousness and buffers one from the disappointment of a
fragile belief system that can lead nowhere, least of all to
answers. It cocoons the vulnerable self against time's disap-
pointments, which can be attributed with ease to the utter
meaninglessness and purposelessness of existence. Nothingness can, however, feel as if it's not a pose at all, since existence can be processed and experienced as truly absurd and
meaningless. Nothing on earth will abide, not even the earth
will endure, so why not believe in nothing? Democritus said

it best: "Nothing means more than nothing." If one reads Sartre, with his being and nothingness — or Hemingway, with his "our nada who art in nada, nada be thy name"; or Shakespeare with his "nothing will come of nothing" in *King Lear*; or Faulkner with his "tale told by an idiot signifying nothing" in *The Sound and the Fury*, via Shakespeare; let alone the prince of nothingness, Samuel Beckett, with his "nothing to be done" — you can believe in nothing.

Yet those imbued with belief in nothingness often paradoxically long for a filling of the void. "I been believing in nothing ever since I was born," the wonderfully named, and self-named, character Manley Pointer — in Flannery O'Connor's "Good Country People" — tells Hulga, the brilliant doctoral student of philosophy who studies nothingness and decides to seduce the young Bible salesman and yokel. He winds up manipulating Hulga into taking off her wooden leg and showing him where it attaches. Then he takes her wooden leg and runs off with it to keep as a souvenir. Hulga, who thinks she believes in nothing, faces someone who really does believe in nothing, with the possible exception of acquiring souvenirs like her wooden leg or selling Bibles he doesn't believe in. Can one truly believe in nothing? Is nothing something? Can we make something of nothing? Should we? Are nothing and something the ultimate antipodes?

I had assimilated enough belief in nothingness that, for a while, as a young professor of literature, I came to believe I believed in nothing, while all along there was well planted in me the desire for something, which, as they say, is surely better than nothing. Nothingness can be alluring — especially to a cerebral young man with a bent toward the romantic and skepticism. But Eliot awakened in me, despite my agnosticism, the desire for something beyond the wasteland of nothingness. I suddenly found myself fairly situated in life, with what Freud, another latter-day Jewish messiah surrogate, said was requisite to happiness — work and love. I was a tenured professor with publications under my belt who relished classroom teaching and loved working with students and pursuing the life of the mind. I was married to a woman I loved, who had borne our first child, whom I watched, with awe and a sense of the miraculous, emerge into life, which made a lie out of my intellectual pose as a nothing man. How could I go on believing I believed in nothing, when love and work and fatherhood and friendship and literature and teaching and scholarship all mattered to me? But again, I had to ask why. Why should they matter? Why should anything matter when all would turn to dust?

I was well-liked, something that had been important to me since boyhood and was tied to my mutating code. I felt I had gone from being a nobody to being a somebody, yet I still needed to find something more, the right occupant to fill my spiritual vacancy and hold off the rising tide of overall nothingness that would continue to well up in me, doubtless due at least in part to reading too many contemporary and postcontemporary writers. My wife, Leslie, recognized in me an ineffable longing — which I hid from others — for a lit spiritual pathway, or spiritual enlightenment, or a mystical awakening, or a seizing of esoteric knowledge, or a visionary moment like the one experienced by one of my students, who had paid a tidy sum to roam the desert with a small troop of vision questers. I hoped a visionary moment would suddenly come on me, or that it was already gestating in me in preparation for a surprise birth. I studied the kabbalah and read and read and read, and I waited and hoped for a mystical moment to sweep me up.

Leslie joked that my searching and longing for a mystical

moment or profound force or belief that would take me over might mean she would awaken one day to find I had become a Chassid, one of those religious, mystical Jews who wear ear-locks and dress in gabardine. Since my Jewish cultural identity had always been strong, my wife entertained the notion that I could perhaps one day cross the threshold into religious Judaism even though agnosticism had become an integral and unbending part of who I was. Once when Leslie and I were in London, in 1979, I woke up early one morning and left our hotel room while she slept. I went for a walk on Bond Street, passed a costume shop, and saw for rent the gabardine coat and other pious accoutrements of the Chassidim. I desperately wanted to rent that costume and put it on, so my wife would wake up and find me standing in it at her bedside. Unfortunately, it was Sunday and the store was closed. But the costume seemed an apt metaphor. If I could take on any kind of religious or mystical garb, it would have to be a costume, as a joke. I was certainly not on a true spiritual pathway. But again, why the need?

I was drawn during my days as a graduate student and rabid reader to *Sartor Resartus*, a novel by the historian Thomas Carlyle. And it is no wonder that I thought again of that unusual novel in London when what could have been a great practical joke on my wife was squelched. *Sartor Resartus* is a satire on the philosophy of clothes and the changing fashions of history, as well as a disputation about language as a garment of thought. A personal code of ethics is, I decided there on Bond Street, a way of dress, the habiliments we choose to clothe ourselves in. I could dress myself as a Chassid for fun, but I could never be one. I could tailor and retailor myself in the robes of many different derivative fashions, wear a kind of patchwork coat of many colors and threads, but I knew I would still need to find a manner of clothing that truly fit me.

I had found work and love and fatherhood, as well as friends I cared for and enjoyed, even cherished. But given the spiritual vacuum I felt, and the feeling of nothingness that came in waves, I suspect I also thought of Carlyle's novel and his protagonist, Diogenes Teufelsdröckh, at that point because Herr Teufelsdröckh was able to move in the novel from an everlasting nay, through a valley of indecision, and ultimately to what Carlyle called an everlasting yea. How could one hope to discover everlasting affirmation in the face of finitude and nothingness? Perhaps transitory affirmations, without a spiritual bedrock, was the most one could hope for.

Spiritual hunger can trump all other hungers and override all feelings of accomplishment and positive affirmations. Examples abound of asceticism in men and women who have fasted, or undertaken a life of celibacy, or in other ways subdued the flesh so the spirit they believed was in them might ascend. I often think of what motivated the Irish political martyr Bobby Sands, who fasted his way to death over sixty-five days in 1981. Or Buddhist monks who set themselves on fire during the war in Vietnam simply to bring public attention to their cause. Or Islamic fanatics who blow themselves up. Where does such self-sacrifice come from, the ability to override or subdue the affirmative power of life for the sake of a higher political or spiritual cause?

The martyrdom of suicide bombers has perplexed many in the West, but I recall reading Allen Tate's great memorial, "Ode to the Confederate Dead," and realizing that Tate was acknowledging the profound belief of those Confederate soldiers who went to their deaths for the Confederacy, sacrificing life for what they believed, for a greater cause than self. One can see martyrdom in all wars in the midst of the many who believe they are dying for a higher purpose or greater reward. The Christ story too is a story of martyrdom, and of the death of a God in human form for a higher spiritual purpose, the redemption of humankind. I didn't want or need such higher rungs of spirituality or a martyr's cause. Just something to fill the spiritual void of nothingness and feed the pangs of spiritual hunger.

Many apparently credible people approach higher consciousness from different perspectives that veer toward the spiritual and reveal that these individuals are driven by what I take to be spiritual hunger. They can wind up cathecting the strange, the weird, the pseudoscientific, or even the implausible. This includes distinguished professionals. Consider the three following distinguished psychiatrists. Harvard psychiatrist John Mack investigated via hypnosis, and lent credence to, the idea of alien abductions. Brian L. Weiss, a Yale medical school graduate and onetime chair of the psychiatry board at Miami's Mount Sinai Medical Center, revealed his belief in reincarnation in the bestselling *Many Lives, Many Masters* and in other popular books. Canadian psychiatrist Ian Stevenson, who researched the medical effects of LSD, as well as reincarnation and near-death experiences, became famous for his work on xenoglossy, an alleged phenomenon in which people with no knowledge of a foreign language find themselves able to speak that language, a result, they believe, of reincarnation.

By most standards these three psychiatrists could be diagnosed as crazy. John Mack was more than a Harvard psychiatrist. He was also a Pulitzer Prize–winning biographer. He became utterly convinced that many men and women he studied had undergone alien abductions. By his account, these were ordinary people with sound minds. Mack characterized their narratives as consistent and credible encounters involving "some sort of visitation." Harvard put Mack and his research under close scrutiny. Critics attacked his thesis that people had been carted off in alien spacecrafts, and challenged his tenure. Mack compared people who believed they had undergone abduction to the state-persecuted Soviet dissidents who had been branded and institutionalized as mentally ill. He insisted they were not psychotic and had clearly undergone an experience in an invisible realm beyond the physical world. Something had occurred — perhaps they had encountered another intelligence or an enhanced or visionary spirituality. These were people who claimed to have undergone sometimes painful physical examinations while aboard space vehicles, and some of their stories were related with a recall marked by stark terror.

Mack pointed to unexplainable disappearances, involving time they could not account for, by a number of those who claimed they had been abducted. He confirmed that there were clear, identifiable marks on the bodies of many of these alleged abductees — cuts, lesions, and other kinds of abrasions. Skeptics like Philip Klass were quick to point out that no abductee had ever brought back an actual souvenir. Other skeptics concluded that the types of experiences recorded and catalogued by Mack had obvious links to present-day science fiction movies, in which extraterrestrials look remarkably like those described by many of the men and women Mack interviewed. This was also a time when mental health professionals were arguing over whether repressed memories of sexual trauma were an actual phenomenon. Memories of abduction were no more verifiable than sudden emergent memories of sexual abuse, but in both cases the emotional effects of reliving the alleged experiences could be unusually intense.

John Mack became convinced that the subjects he studied, some of whom were from remote places where they had little or no exposure to science fiction films, had entered another realm, a third realm beyond the mind and the world as we know it, a realm he likened to the world of the spirit. In response, there was, let us call it, a type of Mack attack. Not only skeptics and academics attacked Mack, but so did the scientific establishment. How could a researcher with Mack's bona fides defy scientific convention and give his imprimatur to such nonsense as abductions by aliens obsessed with exploring human anatomy, with a particular proclivity for penetrating body cavities?

But the abductions seemed inexplicably real to those who claimed to have experienced them, and they soon became real to Mack, though obviously he could never establish certainty. He was looking for answers, feeding his own spiritual hunger and finding purpose, following a path from nowhere to somewhere. He began to hypothesize about reasons for the abductions. If people were being abducted and sexually examined, the purpose appeared to be — and the stories seemed to bear this out — the creation of a new biological hybrid to save the earth in the wake of environmental despoliation. However one ultimately chooses to view Mack and his research, he was filling his own void with questions that led to more questions and, ineluctably, to some tentative answers, which enabled him to traverse a spiritual dimension where he found other answers. John Mack was killed by a drunk driver in 2004.

Brian Weiss and Ian Stevenson too found purpose and answers by entering into what most scientists would categorize as foolish, scientifically unacceptable research. Weiss described himself as a scientist, though his belief in reincarnation and past-life regressions would make that claim laughable to the majority of so-called hard scientists, many of whom look on even traditional psychiatry as a soft science or a pseudoscience. One could easily be cynical about all the money Weiss made from people hungry to believe in what he was vending — which was not only the relief of symptoms through past-life regression therapy but also the kind of message of nonviolence, peace, and love that played well to the Oprah crowd.

I met Weiss a number of years ago and found him to be sincere but naive. He struck me as a nice Jewish boy from New Jersey, though he claimed to have also had past lives as a Catholic priest and a Buddhist priest, and to have started out as a skeptic on his personal odyssey to belief in reincarnation. I learned he had lost a child, and I briefly met his wife, who was wearing a blouse emblazoned with her zodiac sign and who, like him, seemed naive. I understood what had likely turned him to the world of spirit. Nothingness and despair can engulf one after a devastating loss such as the death of a child, but according to Weiss, there is no real death because the spirit never dies. Masters and guides are with us to assist us as we pass through stages of life. Ah, the consolations of spirituality!

I do not want to sound cynical. Agnosticism has a long history of skepticism but not cynicism — though I realize the line between the two can be thin. I can be skeptical about such alleged phenomena as alien abductions and past-life regressions and yet recognize that belief in either or both, even by traditionally trained psychiatrists like Mack and Weiss, could satisfy their spiritual hungers and move them from the despair of nothingness to a higher spiritual consciousness marinated in hope. John Mack and Brian Weiss and those they studied were also likely affected by the zeitgeist of the time, in which people seemingly channeled past lives and expressed interest in such inexplicable occurrences as crop circles and cattle mutilations.

Both Mack and Weiss ultimately delivered unverifiable answers from unseen worlds. Were they psychotic to believe in what they believed? Some would say they were, but Mack discovered what he believed was hope for the planet, and Weiss found consolation for the sorrow of losing his firstborn, as well as supplied consolation to patients who took his exotic brand of therapy to heart. As I've noted, an obsessive search of the realm of the paranormal can simply be another form of the spiritually driven search for meaning.

On the other, darker and truly psychotic, side of this same equation is Major Nidal Malik Hasan, the devout Muslim psychiatrist who slaughtered his fellow soldiers at Fort Hood with Islamic fervor and apparent rage over Muslim deaths in Iraq and Afghanistan. Hasan was about to be deployed to one of those wars. In what sounds like a grotesque form of dark humor, people who knew Hasan revealed that he had been in deep mourning over the death of his parakeet.

Another psychiatrist, the Canadian biochemist and professor of psychiatry Ian Stevenson, who headed the Department of Psychiatry at the University of Virginia, argued that the regressions hypnotically induced by Brian Weiss had to be seen as imagined and unverifiable. But Stevenson, too, believed in reincarnation (as well as near-death experiences, out-of-body experiences, and deathbed visions). He went all over the world, logging more than a million miles over forty years while conducting dogged but highly questionable research. He applied what appeared to him to be rigorous scientific methods to his study of thousands of children possessing birthmarks or defects or memories that he linked to deceased men and women who had lived before the children were born, and who had died violently. Critics scoffed at Stevenson for doing soft science or pseudoscience, and for relying on memories from two- and three-year-old children, whose testimony was no doubt contaminated by the translators he hired and by such factors as confabulation and hidden memory. Stevenson conceded that the evidence for reincarnation was hardly flawless, but he believed in it and remained devoted to the search.

Ultimately, he was certain he had proven false the claim that there is no evidence for reincarnation, but the truth is, there was never any compelling evidence. Some of the details from the lives of these three psychiatrists stand out — such as Brian Weiss's loss of a child and the fact that Ian Stevenson's mother was a theosophist. But the three were rationally schooled and outwardly credible seekers of consciousness whose work crossed into the uncanny and spiritual domains and succeeded in fueling their sense of purpose and releasing the grip of nothingness. These three, and many like them, regardless of training or intelligence or position, were driven by spiritual hunger to pursue paranormal investigations and search for answers to questions that remain unanswerable.

Where does such spiritual hunger come from? Do we simply metabolize spiritual ideas the way we do the food we crave? Hunger for food and sex, I understand, is biological, but I don't understand the source of spiritual hunger, since it often goes beyond the obvious fear or inevitable recognition of our being essentially dying animals. Does it come simply from our awareness that we are infinitesimally small in the vastness of the universe? From our inability to comprehend the unknown or reckon with the incomprehensible? Our need to discover answers? Our need for belief or purpose? Our need to flee uncertainty and nothingness? Or is it encoded in our DNA or the neurotransmitters in our brains?

I speak to some degree for agnostics because I have remained steadfast in my agnosticism despite the sirens of nothingness and my personal cravings for spiritual sustenance. The point is, many agnostics yearn for a spiritual life. Perhaps for me, as for many others, seeking a spiritual life or the path to one is the only answer. I don't know if I have a spiritual life, metaphorically or otherwise. Part of the problem is the signifier. It has become commonplace for men and women these days to call themselves spiritual — which usually seems to connote an association with the divine, or a higher force or power or transcendent purpose, and the recognition (hope?) of the role a life of spirit can play without one necessarily being anchored to religion. If there is no palpable or attainable spirituality, then there is only the mutable and the material, which for many add up to something tantamount to nothing.

I often hear the following statement, which sounds like an example of what Orwell called prefabricated henhouse language: "I'm spiritual but not religious." The religion scholar Huston Smith called attention to the fact that religion is an institution, and institutions are not pretty. He characterized religions as being institutionalized spirituality. Many of today's fallen-away-from-religion types see religion as nothing more than an institution, or they view it as a source of human conflict, misery, sexual repression, confusion, and warring enmity, a refuge for the weak or the money-seeking or for hypocrites and even predatory perverts. Yet religion and spirituality can and do provide comfort, solace, meaning, and morality, even inner peace.

Spirituality in today's marketplace of ideas usually follows along the lines of opening up one's heart to a higher force, or discovering how one's life follows a higher purpose, or how everything, even suffering and despair, can be a harbinger of or a prelude to enlightenment. Perhaps as an academic colleague of mine, the philosopher Jacob Needleman, says, today's spirituality is simply a search for truth. But in today's parlance, spirituality also appears to have strong links to detachment from ego and a merging of material consciousness with inner consciousness that can mirror and unite with the transcendent, the divine, the eternal, the Atman, and bring satori. The discovery of inner truth is for many the way out of nothingness.

I have witnessed firsthand and watched on film the manifold effects of the varieties of spiritual satiety, the passions, the zeal, the energy of pure delight, that Blake wrote about. Oh ye of colossal faith! Ye who know nothing of nothingness! Spiritual acolytes and spiritual devotees, I have observed you from the sidelines as the spirit, or whatever you choose to name it, took you over and moved you, filled you up. I have watched Hari Krishnas dance and chant on street corners and in airports, losing themselves in the ecstasy of higher spiritual consciousness, bathing in the electric and electrifying spirit of divine love they felt jolt through them. I took in the looks of ecstasy in the eyes of the born-again filling a stadium with their hunger for Jesus, a hunger Billy Graham adeptly fed as spiritually ravenous Christ lovers left their seats and marched forward to accept Graham's vision of Jesus Christ and the spiritual reward the preacher assured them went with taking Christ into their hearts as their Lord and savior.

I stared at the rapidly blinking Joel Osteen preaching to his enthralled, megasized television audience, delivering a message about the absolute certainty of God's miraculous powers, about how God could do anything for them or their loved ones, whatever the faithful hoped or prayed for, if they only would recognize his love for them and cleave to him. I have seen the bowing-toward-Mecca Muslim pilgrims in Islamic garb quivering in certainty that Allah had found passage to their souls. I have heard Muslims pronounce with deep piety the name of their holy prophet, Mohammed, and the automatic "peace be unto him" that rapidly follows the utterance of the name of Allah's messenger. I interviewed the Hindu holy man Sri Sri Ravi Shankar on stage in front of thousands, a gentle, frail, bearded guru whom the faithful believed could answer any question they sought an answer to. They wanted simply to be in what they discerned as his radiant presence, to feel his spiritual touch or merely to be seen by him. They believed contact with him or wisdom imparted by him could feed their hearts, widen their souls, still their inner torment, and stay their rampant spiritual hunger. I saw thousands rapt with attention while I, as an interlocutor seated on stage, elicited sage rhetorical guideposts for life from Buddhist teachers Pema Chödrön and Jack Kornfield. I observed followers of the Dalai Lama gazing at him with awe and veneration and feasting on his Tibetan words; many looked on him as they would a living, incarnate God.

I saw the followers of the Reverend Moon staring and holding their breath while their self-proclaimed messiah spoke passionately in Korean, rather than in a messianic tongue like Hebrew or Aramaic; and I bore witness to the zealous awe- and veneration-filled followers of Rabbi Schneerson, the *chassidic* messiah with a prostate problem, whom many of those Lubavitchers still believe will rise from his grave. I sat in an auditorium watching as those who sat with me in utter silence, starved for words from their dead loved ones, listened with passionate intensity while a charlatan spiritualist minister, his eyes half shut and fluttering, spoke in a high falsetto that the entire flock believed was the voice of their dear ones coming through him from beyond the grave. I watched as young American men and women clamored to enter Native American sweat lodges to embrace an Indian spirituality unconnected to their own bloodlines or personal histories. I observed Polish youth in Kraków dancing horas to frenetic klezmer music and chomping on falafel — all raised Catholic but longing for remnants of Jewish spirituality, which the Nazis and their Polish cohorts had nearly erased from Poland.

I watched as Gerald Jampolsky, of attitudinal healing fame, called on his dewy-eyed faithful to clasp hands and feel the power of healing course miraculously through them. I watched the ecstasy, the thrilled responses of the moneyed flock of American Buddhists as they gazed with awe on *rinpoches*, as kids did at Woodstock on the Grateful Dead and Jimi Hendrix. I saw throngs of men and women craning to see, for the briefest of seconds, the figure of Pope John Paul as he sat regally encased in his so-called popemobile. One can belittle the joys and ecstasies, the awe and trembling, the comforting certainties, the many varieties of spirituality that sit on the faithful and the gullible, the devout and the naive, the pious and the foolish. But I envy those feelings. They can fill the inner void, the emptiness of being, the tunnel without light through which we all must travel. They can give comfort, satiety, peace. I crave such feelings for they are feelings of enlightenment, of certainty, of purpose. They can dispel for a lifetime the feelings of nothingness and worthlessness. They can transfigure. They can attach one to the reassuring umbilicus of belief, and they can bring forth hope.

Much spirituality today is the faith of the so-called New

Age, the by-product of the dawn of Aquarius and of ongoing secularization and loss of faith in organized and institutional religious worship and belief. After all the time I spent at Esalen Institute in Big Sur, a place where all forms of Eastern philosophy are taught to and practiced by some of America's privileged class, I realized that many of those who were there, walking alongside me or in the dappled gardens, or sitting with me naked in the tubs overlooking the ocean, were pilgrims in search of spiritual nourishment. I discovered evanescent moments of peace at Esalen, a place surrounded by the spectacular beauty of Big Sur and situated on the once holy land of the Esalen Indians. But I also felt afflicted there with spiritual envy, because, though I have longed for years for spiritual knowledge or a mystical, pure spiritual experience, I doubt the search and I doubt the rewards.

Agnostic doubt precludes any certainty of discovering a way to satiate spiritual hunger. One can, of course, be spiritual without being New Age. And one can embrace the underlying tenets of an organized religion without following all its customs, and can consider that to be spiritual rather than religious. But spiritual envy includes envy not only of those who have found answers or who practice a spirituality that yields sustenance but also those who believe they are on a path or engaged in a practice that will lead to answers, who have set out to discover the spiritual territory within, sure of, or at least hopeful of, finding the spiritual vein of ore to mine and the tools to mine it.

There are even those who have theorized that Freud envied religious experience, that his early feelings of maternal deprivation and disappointment with his father as a provider were what accounted for his envy and compulsion to spoil the "good object" that existed in the minds of others in the form of religious experience. He wrote, in his famous letter to the French novelist Romain Rolland, of his lack of capacity for oceanic feelings. Intimations of the loss of oceanic feeling — which Freud likened to an infant's inability to separate himself or herself from feelings of oneness with the breast — can create envy even in a hardened agnostic breast. One can long for the oceanic, for God's presence, for grace or enlightenment. Yearning to surrender spiritual doubt is like the yearning to surrender to love, and can be as profound.

Rudolf Steiner, who espoused the idea of overriding the dualism of the material and spiritual, or of faith and science, believed we possess a spiritual appetite, and that the desire to understand meaning in the universe is comparable to our biological hunger and thirst. Advances in neuroscience point to a spiritual part of the brain, to neural regions that, when given electrical stimulation, bring strong feelings of spirituality and communication with God. A number of nonbelieving scientists see this as evidence that God is a creation of humankind, while believers in God argue that the infinitely wise creator provided, in the brain, a center for our spirituality.

Years ago a philosophy professor named Philip Clayton asked me to moderate some discussions featuring a group of world-class scientists at Harvard on the topic of science and the spiritual quest. The conference was funded by the billionaire philanthropist and lifelong Presbyterian Sir John Templeton, who has devoted great sums of money to the scientific exploration of faith and spirituality. Though the conference was free of overt religious identification, it was held at the venerable Trinity Church in Cambridge, Massachusetts. An international array of distinguished and award-winning scientists offered biological and other physical scientific evidence of a range of possible connections to a higher order, to a force beyond our own. The result of various scientific methodologies and explorations, this evidence yields suggestions of the spiritual realm or dimension, of a metaphysics linked to the physical or biological sciences.

The conference participants grappled with finding points of consonance between theoretical insights of modern science and the teachings of the world's religious traditions, and with demonstrating parallels between practices and disciplines of science and diverse practices and disciplines of spirituality. The scientists took on central questions, such as what is consciousness and how can spiritual perspectives enhance the scientific quest, and they speculated on what the opportunities and challenges were likely to be in the revolutions in information technology, nanotechnology, neuroscience, and genomics. I left the event excited by a lot of what I learned, but unconvinced of a convergence between science and spirituality, and with all my doubts intact. I don't believe science and faith need be seen as mutually exclusive, particularly by any scientists who happen to be of firm faith. One can believe in both. Many of these brilliant attendees obviously did. Still, though I was intellectually stimulated by what many of them had to offer, and had hoped for something of higher meaning to emerge, I was unpersuaded from my agnosticism. I did, however, feel spiritually envious of the scientists who felt they had discovered or confirmed spiritual essence via their telescopes, microscopes, and computers, and, I ought to add, I envied the courage shown in their willingness to take a religious or spiritual stand, which often raises skepticism and disapproval in scientific and academic circles.

The American public is crowded with spiritual seekers — they are Oprah-watching devotees of kitsch spirituality, or the followers of self-proclaimed spiritual teachers of *The Secret*, which is a reworking of Norman Vincent Peale's *The Power of Positive Thinking* connected to ideas of vibrations and energy. Or they are students of spiritual teachers like Eckhart Tolle, Marianne Williamson, and Rabbi Michael Lerner, who write out of a serious commitment to establishing directives concerning spiritual consciousness appealingly and fashionably tied to ecology, feminism, and a basic philosophy of changing one's internal spiritual landscape in order to merge with the deeper and wider expanse of the living universe. Then we have the range of more professionally and scientific-trained thinkers who also see convergence between the inner world and the outer that defies the Cartesian division, including the physicist Fritjof Capra of *The Tao of Physics* fame, who posits interrelatedness and unity of the universe, and unity of Eastern mysticism and quantum theory. Or Cambridge-trained biologist Rupert Sheldrake, with his noetic explorations of morphic fields and extended-mind hypothesis, or Buddhist philosopher and author Ken Wilber, with his integral theory of consciousness.

Much of the wave of recent forms of spirituality that has hit the United States and spread globally has evolved from Eastern philosophy and from early views of holistic health that morphed from mind-body unity into notions of spiritual sustenance seen as vital to maintaining optimal fitness and physical health. Ecological and psychological theories abound that tie spiritual consciousness to creating balance on earth as well as in the human psyche. Innovative New Age medical doctors like Dean Ornish, Deepak Chopra, and Andy Weil, who have data to back them up (though *New Yorker* science writer Michael Specter, for one, has blasted a good deal of Weil's data, calling it specious), promulgate spirituality as a central building block in physical and mental health and

greater longevity. Spirituality or faith might increase my actu-
arial possibilities and benefit my personal health, but I remain
an agnostic, a spiritual wallflower on the sidelines watching
and absorbing and learning without the willingness or ability
to cast off doubt and skepticism and join in the dance. I remain
a kind of Kafkaesque spiritual hunger artist — essentially not
liking or desiring what is out there in the spiritual troughs,
like the hunger artist who simply did not like the food.

And yet I remain envious of those who graze there, and
not just for their potentially better health and greater longevity. I would welcome a spiritual regimen, to feel spiritual nourishment or satiety or simply to discover an abiding or even
an evanescent faith, to experience transcendence or simply
to feel the drive to seek enlightenment or follow after some
trustworthy pied piper of spirituality, a guru or master strong
enough to bend my cognition as well as my will. Unfortunately, as Gertrude Stein said of her one-time Oakland home,
there is no there there, at least not for me and doubtless not for
legions of adults with similar spiritual blockage. I used to joke
as my father crossed into octogenarianism that his reading the
Bible at that stage of life was his way of studying for his final
exams. He was a man who believed in God and who liked to
quote the line by the Hebrew prophet Micah about the good
Lord wanting us to do justice, love mercy, and walk humbly
with God. My dad was a scientist by training and a man of
considerable wisdom. I wanted to ask him as he came closer
to death how one could walk humbly with God if God's presence could not be known.

To believe fully in God's ultimate power would mean
one believed God could do anything, and my father never, to
my knowledge, even in his dementia, stopped believing. But
if God existed as the personal, caring God I spoke intimately

with in my God-loving boyhood, why could I not enlist him to help my declining father? How many, I wonder, have lost their faith in God because of unanswered prayers sent to enlist God's aid in healing or diminishing pain or sustaining the life of a loved one? Just help me, Oh Lord, and I promise I will be good and do all that you command. I will not trespass. I will not ask for anything else of you. Is God not both the quintessential wishing well and the überdealmaker? When the seemingly miraculous does occur, how can we possibly verify whether it is connected to faith and the power of God or to a spiritual force beyond us? Yet spiritual faith anchored in certainty offers a wonderful payoff — a bulwark against meaninglessness and death. Deals are made with God, and if remission occurs or the heart continues beating or the infant doesn't drown, the human dealmaker must decide if he or she will keep the promise made to God.

The many who adhere to the often vague spirituality of the Age of Aquarius, as well as those fortunate enough to possess the considerable faith of ages past, can resign themselves to death with the comforting notion that everything actually does happen for a reason, even if the reason remains shrouded in mystery and the dead tell no audible tales. I knew, unfortunately at a young age, that we were deceived if we believed a guiding hand was behind tragedy or that faith could move the cold hand of death, let alone mountains.

Chapter 10

RESPECT FOR THE FAITHFUL,
THE FAITHLESS, AND
THE WISHY-WASHY

gnostics cannot help knowing they do not know, and must remain in the temporal limbo of uncertainty, where they cannot say for sure if God's Ten Commandments, or anything else that is God's, is actually God's. The Bible had its human authors. Yet fundamentalists and others who fervently believe that the Bible is the word of God, not merely a potpourri of stories and observations and myths, recognize it as God's word and the human authors who wrote it as having been guided by God (which would make God the world's bestselling ghostwriter). Atheists and agnostics, even theistic agnostics like the nineteenth-century philosopher and evolutionist Herbert Spencer, flatly reject the Bible as the word of God. Agnostics may yearn for God or paternal or spiritual sustenance or transcendence, but agnostics remain waiting. We are like Keats's youthful lover chasing the young woman on the Grecian urn in suspended Attic time, not catching or holding what seems never to stop eluding us.

Before my children were born, I prayed they would be born healthy. It was a throwback, I knew, to my childhood and my early dependency on God, to my fear of the unknown and my recognition of what fate could cruelly spawn. I needed phantom assurance from a higher power helping out with the birth and ensuring the health of my children in spite of my doubts, my skepticism, my intellectual reasoning that contradicted God's presence in my life or anyone else's. But how could I be sure when both my daughters were born healthy (thank God!) that there wasn't divine oversight? How could I know? I didn't buy, but I didn't dismiss. Wishy-washy agnostic! I felt on the one hand as if I should give thanks for blessings and what seemed the miracle of birth, and on the other that I was being absurdly primitive and irrational, even cowardly, in having such mixed emotions.

I also recognized that I longed, on some deep level where my spiritual hunger rested, to stay true and loyal to the God I had lost, the God of my boyhood, particularly if, by whatever invisible power beyond my deep skepticism, he was still looking after me or judging me or waiting for some entrance back into my life. I apologized for going so long without praying — since the Cuban missile crisis — and I believed and I didn't believe. The part of me that believed wanted my good credit intact. The part of me that didn't wanted what Emerson might have called a foolish consistency. The believer might righteously point out that such vestigial fears are intimations or even evidence of a higher and undeniable consciousness.

I recall the shock I experienced on first encountering Madalyn Murray O'Hair. She was the woman who filed suit in 1963 to stop mandatory school prayer on the grounds that it was unconstitutional. The case went all the way to the U.S. Supreme Court, and O'Hair, an atheist who founded American

Atheists, and who was later murdered by one of her atheist followers, was victorious and infamous. She got tagged as "the most hated woman in America." I remember thinking, if one loves God, one obviously has to hate a person like O'Hair who says there is no God. But I could not hate her, not only because my own belief was faltering but also because I operated under the assumption that everyone had a right to believe what he or she wanted to believe.

I believed in that notion from boyhood on while attempting to establish a code of my own. It was perfectly consonant with the idea of religious tolerance on which the American republic was established, a nation first begun by persecuted, and eventually persecuting, Puritan zealots. As I became more estranged from organized religion, I still felt my code had to include respect for people's right to believe whatever they chose to believe. Religion was an instrument of intolerance, violence, and often rank stupidity, but it seemed to me that belief also offered hope for many, as well as moral suasion to resist evil. Concerning Madalyn Murray O'Hair, I wondered how she could find a solid moral base. It was my first inkling that godlessness could possibly mean moral relativism. And godlessness was then, of course, synonymous with communism. But I folded into my code my mother and father's early caveat to me, repeated throughout my childhood, to respect the beliefs of others regardless of how odd they might be as long as they were not harmful.

There are those who see agnosticism or atheism as doing harm because their own faiths or beliefs seem paramount. I respect that to a point, but should it interfere to any degree with my convictions or my free expression, then a Rubicon has been crossed. One principle to which I have held fast is not to belittle or be contemptuous of the faith of others, even a faith that seems outrageous or absurd to me. This is sometimes difficult, because a good deal of nonsense and hypocrisy passes for faith, or for belief, and serious malignancy, cruelty, and horror too often spring from faith and belief, whether tied to religion or to doctrinaire political ideology, such as that associated with mass murderers who were Marxist offshoots — Stalin, Mao, Pol Pot, Ceausescu. Murderous tyrants also do good deeds. Is a large part of their motivation political? Of course. What passes for a good deed is often just a way to win hearts and minds. Dictators like Mao and Castro and Ahmadinejad, and groups like Hezbollah in Lebanon and Hamas in Gaza, help build capital and credibility by helping with literacy and health care and aiding those in poverty, but that will to do good can also be fueled by beliefs.

When Susan Sontag caused a stir by announcing that communism is fascism, she was recognizing what many felt, that the central ideologies of both the left and the right had done great harm. The same can be said of the religions of the East and West. But part of my code has been to allow for the infinite human differences my mother believed were all part of God's handiwork, and to recognize that one should respect what people find meaningful and important. In other words, I respect the fact that others do not see as I see or feel as I feel or believe as I believe (or don't believe). One of the great virtues of the American republic has been its tolerance of faiths of many stripes and hues, a tradition that extends, as I've indicated, back to the Puritans who came to these shores to escape religious persecution, though they zealously took up the practice themselves, even killing en masse nonbelievers, Native Americans, and so-called witches.

Should one respect the beliefs of others even if they seem

ludicrous or absurd, or if they present possible, even imminent, harm? Obviously not. But respect for religious traditions and faith stems from the Enlightenment and ought to include historic awareness of all who suffered because of religious extremism, without excusing the violence of any subsequent form of religious extremism. Blackening religion because of its iniquitous, bloody history of persecution, oppression, and violence is unacceptable as an absolute. There is a wonderful tradition of good deeds and the creation of magnificent art tied to religious faith. Many have sought to live eleemosynary or ethical lives and have given their lives to higher and nobler callings out of a sense of duty to their religious beliefs.

Catholicism inspired not only the building of the world's great cathedrals but also the Polish Solidarity Movement and Liberation Theology. What would Gandhi be without Hinduism? Malcolm X (El-Hajj Malik El-Shabazz) without Islam? Martin Luther King without Christianity? What would America have become without its Puritan work ethic?

Were it not for people of faith and their institutions in the United States, we likely would not have had successful abolition and civil rights movements. There were doubtless atheists and agnostics in both movements, and post-Enlightenment concerns over issues of social justice might have prompted people to act in any case. But the momentum of both movements came from religious believers and the institutions they built, often — in the case of the abolition movement both in the United States and western Europe — in direct opposition to the status quo that allowed slavery. The altruistic deeds prompted by core religious beliefs, and the generosity of spirit that belief in God has inspired in multitudes, are as far beyond calculation as the horror and carnage religion has caused. Religion and spirituality have sparked moral advancement and ethical action at the same time that they have wrought devastating and inestimable harm.

My recognition of the positive, constructive side of religion, both in individuals' personal lives and in the larger moral and political spheres, makes me feel discomfort when I see religion attacked, as it is, for example, in Bill Maher's *Religulous*. The film is laugh-out-loud funny in parts, but its main purpose is to ridicule what the clever satirist and lapsed Catholic Maher views as the nonsensical and toxic character of organized religions throughout the ages and in our present day. Obviously religion can be toxic. And that dimension makes good fodder for satire. Respect, put simply, obliges those to whom it is given to act responsibly. But should we not respect, really respect, what others believe, especially when belief can sow good?

Would that I could know God as the faithful do, or reject him out of hand like the faithless. Or better yet, talk to him as Moses was alleged to have done. Simply knowing God or feeling his presence can bring peace as well as hasten great personal accomplishment. And it can infuse one with an extraordinary power. While watching the 2008 Olympics, which took place in Beijing, I followed a front-page story about the controversial Kisik Lee, head coach of the U.S. archery team, who had become a spiritual guide for athletes who trained and lived at the Olympic Training Center, even baptizing a young competitor weeks before the games began. This evident proselytizing alarmed the United States Olympic Committee, but the fact is, faith can fuel peak performance and prompt extraordinary feats.

The 1981 film *Chariots of Fire*, scripted by Colin Welland, is full of historic inaccuracies but nevertheless accurately portrays the reverent and future reverend Eric Liddell. "The Flying Dutchman," as Liddell was called, refused to violate the commandment to rest on the Sabbath day, opting not to run in one of the 1924 Olympic races, scheduled on a Sunday, that he was slated to compete in. Liddell says, in the scriptwriter's memorable words, "God made me fast, and when I run, I feel His pleasure." The film suggests not only that Liddell sees his speed as a gift from God but also that God truly takes pleasure in Liddell's running. His sense of God is related to the phenomenal burst of speed that brings him the gold in the race in which he does compete.

When I worked with prisoners years ago at San Quentin as a teacher and lecturer, I discovered that those best able to face their future with determination, rather than fall into recidivist criminal behavior or other pathologies of the sort that accounted for their being incarcerated in the first place, were often those who felt they had discovered and knew the Lord. They had made a commitment to God, or found Jesus as their personal savior, or, in the case of many black prisoners, had converted to Islam or become Black Muslims like Malcolm X. That is another reason why I do not derogate spiritual faith even though, as religion's detractors are quick, and correct, to point out, religion — or at least those who have acted in its name — may indeed be responsible for the greatest amount of torture and greatest number of imposed, as well as conflict-related, deaths in all of human history. Notwithstanding the horrors religion has wrought, it can render what appears to be a miraculous kind of power to perform good works or defeat adversity. Knowing and feeling God, as has been demonstrated repeatedly by so-called faith healers, can make crippled men throw away their crutches and old women rise out of wheelchairs they have been in for years.

The dependence on a higher power that is integral to the 12-step program has had results, despite the naysayers who cite statistics revealing that many fall back into their addictions. Religion can make people kill and torture and abuse and otherwise deny human rights, but it can also compel them to perform deeds of great charity and generosity. Which is probably why more people of faith donate blood than do nonbelievers. Think of the religious men and women who risked their lives to save others from the brutal Nazis. And knowing and feeling God can also help one carry on and endure.

Since I cannot know or feel God, I would settle for simply being able to communicate with him. There are many questions I would like answered, many lifetime curiosities and concerns — some raised over the course of writing this book — that could be put to rest if God would only assure me of his divine presence and let me know, via my senses, that what I might see or hear of him is real. What a fantastical thought, to imagine God speaking directly to me! (Richard Pryor, early in his career, did a bit in which a black preacher tells of first meeting God while "eating a tuna fish sandwich" and walking along on the boardwalk of Atlantic City. He hears God's voice, holy and resounding, asking for "a bite of that tuna fish sandwich.")

But of course, God does not speak to me. Yet I can accept that others hear the voice of God without my needing to condemn or ridicule them or see them as nuts. They are fortunate to have found answers, when all my adult life has been troubled by questions. If no higher power answers my questions, or my questions are not answered by a sudden, intuitive realization (which surely cannot be scientifically trusted), then I am bound to keep questioning, destined to remain in doubt.

Most religious beliefs seem foolish and nearly primitive to

me, and there can be serious harm done in the name of faith, as in cases where Christian Scientist parents adamantly refuse lifesaving medical help for their children out of a devout belief in God's powers of intervention. But among nonbelievers, who often believe in their intellectual superiority, are some who have general contempt for those who hold religious beliefs. We live in an era of dogmatic and proselytizing atheism. At an event where I introduced Richard Dawkins to the audience, the audience responded wildly, as if I were introducing a rock star. Dawkins is in many ways a brilliant man. But he is also as dogmatic in his atheistic beliefs, and as set on spreading them, as many of the implacably religious, true-believer types, and like some of them, he has many acolytes.

And what of beliefs not based on religion? The same principle applies. I think astrology is absurd and give it no credence, but millions believe their lives are ruled by the stars. Not a whit of it, like most religious belief, has a valid scientific basis. Many skeptics point out that astrology is irrational, perhaps even dangerous. Foolish and irrational, yes, but not likely dangerous unless misused on the gullible for some sinister or venal purpose. But why not tolerate those who believe in astrology, and reduce the contempt? Cut them slack. I need not be contemptuous of someone who asks me what my sign is and believes his or hers or mine controls destiny. That person might think less of me, and perhaps think me mad because I do not arrange my life according to the horoscope charts, just as religious believers might think me misguided or contemptible for being an agnostic. But we can all maintain a benign tolerance for what others believe, as long as they, like physicians, obey the Hippocratic imperative and do no harm.

Chapter 11

ACCURSED TIME

*W*hen I was studying for my doctorate in literature at the University of Wisconsin in Madison, Wisconsin, and falling deeper into love with Leslie and literature, the children of a woman who lived next door to me randomly wreaked havoc on my car with baseball bats for no reason other than because they were destructive, had too much time on their hands, and were unsupervised. The woman told me when I sought payment from her for repairs to my car that each of her five ragamuffin sons had a different father, three sons had physical or mental disabilities, and another had swallowed a nickel and had to be hospitalized for a surgical procedure, for which she had no insurance. She had lung cancer, and her most recent lover had left her only hours before I came to talk to her about the damage done to my car. "Why should I go on?" she abruptly asked me. "Tell me why I should go on." I thought involuntarily about God and the gift of life, and I instantly recoiled at the thought. There was nothing I could offer this poor woman that would ease her suffering or give her a reason to go on living what to her was clearly a depressing life. I couldn't ask her for any money, and I had no words for her.

Despite my spiritual hunger, I felt fairly content in those years, though I knew that the Buddha was right to have seen life, despite its intermittent joys, as tied ultimately and ineluctably to suffering. If one were to internalize the suffering of others and literally feel their pain, as I did to some degree for the mother of those ragamuffins, one could wind up going off the rails like Nathanael West's character Miss Lonelyhearts. The newspaper advice columnist, a man writing under a feminine byline, encounters irremediable human suffering in the nevertheless darkly comedic letters he receives from advice seekers, like the sixteen-year-old girl who is born without a nose and looks at herself all day and cries, but claims to be a good dancer. Suffering is not only ubiquitous, it is also inseparable from the human condition because of aging and decay and mortality — and, as the Buddha wisely noted, because of separation from that which we love, and being conjoined with what we do not or cannot love.

I first read about Buddhism and suffering when I was a high school student. I asked my parents, as we sat eating Chinese food at Cedar Center's China Gate, in Cleveland, why life had to be impermanent and why I had to face the certainty of their deaths as well as my own. My mother had this hypothetical question she would throw at me at times during my boyhood. She would pose a scenario in which she and my father were in a sinking boat with just me and my wife, and I could save only one of the three. I would protest that it was a dumb question because I didn't have a wife then, and I dearly loved both of them. What kind of choice was that to have to make anyway? To me, there was no right answer. My mother would reassuringly and without hesitation tell me there was indeed a right answer, and it was that I should save my wife, because my parents had done their job of having and raising their children, and the younger generation was what mattered. She repeated this question, and the same answer, to me for years, in different ways, as if I were being catechized. But when I asked my parents why life had to be impermanent, why nothing of what we call material reality or mortal life can last, my mother simply said, "Honey, I wish we knew."

Time is the real metaphysical riddle, is it not? Time is the crusher, the destroyer, the inescapable, and the ineluctable. It can be the healer of loss and emotional wounds too, of course; but time, it seems, is the key. Not so much how we manage it, but how it gels and how it fits or doesn't fit into our consciousness. "God is a jigsaw timer," sang Laura Nyro in one of those songs from my youth in Madison that to this day can elevate me and stir my emotions. Moses may have seen God's backside while on top of Mount Sinai, but, according to scripture, Moses was also able to see the promised land. Sadly enough, the Bible says he never trod on it. There apparently was not time, and God was angry at Moses for not speaking to the rock or trusting God. If you are a believer, you must ask why God would not permit Moses, their greatest prophet and leader, to step onto the land promised to the children of Israel. The story of Moses dying before reaching the promised land is a cautionary tale. Death, despite what the poet Dylan Thomas said, has dominion. We age. We die. There is, as Wallace Stevens pointed out in his sermon poem "Sunday Morning," no "imperishable bliss." Or as Hemingway put it in his terse way: "All stories end in death."

Even Augustine seemed agnostic about time when he asked, back in the fifth century, "What, then, is time?" and answered, "If no one ask of me, I know. But if I wish to explain to him who asks, I know not." We can feel time just as we can feel spiritual hunger, but it is nearly impossible to explain time in a way that truly elucidates. I remember when I first read Camus' definition of what he called eternal nothingness. It went along the lines of how we should try to imagine what life will mean five thousand years from now. And years before I read Camus, I read Bertrand Russell's remark that everything that makes up our lives, and all the history we have established and have memory and records of, could have been created but a mere instant, an eyeblink, ago. How could we prove that everything preceding our existence — including the fossils, ancient documents on papyrus, cave scrawlings, and yesterday's news — did not come into being, were not all created, in the last nanosecond? In time's flux there is no real *ago*. There is no permanence. There is only the present moment, the now that T. S. Eliot said is always now. What memory stores is diminished or lost in time. In time's flux we are all doomed to oblivion and to die for the birth we did not invite.

Bertrand Russell said, "To realize the importance of time is the gate to wisdom." Is time an illusion? What does it mean to be told by today's physicists that time emerged originally from quantum foam or vibrating strings? As a boy, I walked along a small bridge in Painesville, Ohio, at a summer camp where I went through a difficult time because of enuresis, or as it is more commonly called, bed-wetting. It was an experience right out of *Lord of the Flies* — boys in my tent discovered I was a bed wetter and taunted me in the merciless way boys do, with almost demonic energy. I was nine years old, and I was terribly unhappy. I wanted desperately to go home, but I couldn't leave the camp until two more of the paid-for three weeks had gone by.

As I crossed over that bridge, I thought to myself how

hard it would be to get past the two weeks to come, that those days would seem to last forever. I was well aware even then of evanescence. I was aware that time would pass, and that there would be a time when I would remember that moment as part of the past. The bridge crossing would become part of memory. A bridge! How apt! Like a nascent Proust, I told myself to remember the moment as vividly as possible, the moment spent crossing that particular bridge, so that I could resurrect the memory at some point in my future. That fleeting moment of cognition of what was then the present would be recalled in what was to be my future, and in years to come would emerge in what Proust identified as voluntary and involuntary memory.

More than a half century has passed, and I still bring that moment back — or the moment suddenly and unpredictably makes an entrance. To what extent is bringing back a moment illusory, as memory finds the pathway back to my childhood more and more elusive? I recall, too, thinking that I felt I was . outside myself, a feeling that was surreal then and remains surreal in memory. "All of life is a dream," my mother used to like saying in Yiddish when contemplating the rapid passage of time, especially after spending time away from Cleveland in California with my brother and me and our families. My father would say, after being with us in California, "The time goes faster than a jet plane." Both of my parents, simple Jewish peasants, knew full well what it was to feel the thrust of time, the sheer speed, the unreality, the propulsion that moves through us like that green fuse Dylan Thomas wrote about, what he saw as God's, or nature's, hand:

> The hand that whirls the water in the pool
> Stirs the quicksand; that ropes the blowing wind
> Hauls my shroud sail.

If we are imprisoned by time, then God, if he exists, is our jailer and perhaps also our warden. Agnosticism carries with it the not-so-startling realization that, if there is a Governor, he cannot or will not necessarily grant a stay of execution. Time may make fools of us all, but it also murders us. If time is my destroyer and God exists, then God is time made manifest, "the bloody tyrant time," as Shakespeare called it. Charlie Chaplin, whose father read Robert Ingersoll at the age of seventeen and encouraged his son to read the great agnostic, said that time was his only enemy. Chaplin was probably, toward the end of his life, an agnostic like his father (his mother was very religious), though in his autobiography he acknowledged his belief in a "supreme force" and in a "fixed purpose beyond the comprehension of our three-dimensional minds." Still, if time was his sole enemy, then the supreme force, the force that drives the flower and the water through rocks and our blood, was indeed the relentless, strangling hands of time.

Both Chronos, the Greek personification of time, and the figure of Father Time, who is connected to Chronos, are often, like God, pictured as old men with flowing beards — though Chronos was earlier a three-headed God with the heads of a man, a bull, and a lion. *Chronos* means "time," and the name of the figure associated with him, *Aeon*, means "eternal time" or "God." Theologians of the West appear to agree that God brought space into being, but there is ongoing disagreement about whether God is eternal and not in time at all, or eternal even if temporal. In Stephen Hawking's model of the universe, there is no role for the creator, because there is no exact time when the universe began. This is a position many of deep faith would find comforting, at least for the absence of specific timing for what they accept as the handiwork of God, the master of time. Christians who believe in God and his kingdom believe he can grant eternal life, can give us doomed mortals the most precious gift, the vanquishing of time, a result of his having given up his most precious possession — his only begotten son.

In time's flux I can, for now, no more know eternity than I can death or God. Eternity remains as distant from my consciousness, as unreachable and unknowable, as God in his heaven or as the full realization, with what Cardinal Newman called emotional assent, of my death and what it will mean. I assume death means the end of consciousness, and that souls neither actually exist nor transmigrate, but as with most matters of agnostic thought, I don't really know because I cannot.

How can we not long for a sense of timelessness that reaches upward toward the idea of the eternal or toward the everlasting, toward freedom from subjugation by what Pozzo in *Waiting for Godot* calls "accursed time"? When elevated, I feel time's burden less if at all; I hear not the winged chariot at my back. I try in moments of elevation or, better yet, moments of unbridled joy to be in those moments and not think of their soon being gone. The thought of time's flux brings the shadow of impermanence. When I was a young graduate student and professor, love and literature and friendship and art and food and music were my battlements against time. Leslie and I went to see the popular singer Jim Croce in 1973, the year before his death, at age thirty, in a plane crash. Consider these lines from "Time in a Bottle," one of Croce's best-known songs:

If I could save time in a bottle
The first thing that I'd like to do
Is to save every day

Till eternity passes away
Just to spend them with you

Chorus: But there never seems to be enough time
To do the things we want to do
Once you find them
I've looked around enough to know
That you're the one I want to go
Through time with.

Croce's early death is painfully ironic in light of this song, and the song is a sweet testament to youthful romantic love and the idealization of an unnamed woman by the songwriter, who puts her beyond time and even eternity. But the notion that we can even imagine what it would be like to control time and its ravages, or to cross the threshold into reckoning with any understanding of eternity — such a notion is perhaps the best testament of why time truly does make fools of us all. We all feel bound by time, but paradoxically, we experience, even in the absence of faith and when overridden by doubt, moments of elevation and joy that seem to release us from time's clutches and place us, or seem to place us, beyond it in a seeming presentness that can feel transcendent. We can speculate and dream of life everlasting, since death remains an undiscoverable terrain. Can the mind actually wrap itself around the concept of eternity? We move through our lives assured of death within our temporality, and yet paradoxically and almost comically feel as if we are beyond the certitude of death. It is understandable why many spiritual teachers view the examination of time as the truly spiritual practice.

Who is that child walking across the camp bridge in 1953? Can he exist in memory only? Did he ever really exist? Wordsworth said, "The child is father of the man," and Yeats said we cannot tell the dancer from the dance. Is that child still alive inside me? Is that child merely an artifact of a memory losing the neurons that cause it to exist, a memory that is entropic — physicists tell us the entire universe is entropic — declining in accuracy as the body ages and time relentlessly moves forward? That child crossing the bridge knows nothing of the questing or questioning or doubting of God or Moses or God's commandments or the perplexity of impossible-to-answer metaphysical questions or the enigmas of time and eternity. That child knows that God is in his heaven even if all is not right with the child's world. That child's thoughts are given over mostly to wanting two weeks to be behind rather than ahead of him. Baudelaire said, "Don't be martyred slaves of time," but such a concept is not in that child's head and, as I think of that child, Eliot's words in "Burnt Norton," the first of the four quartets, echo in my adult mind:

Time present and time past
Are both perhaps present in time future,
And the future contained in time past.
If all time is eternally present
All time is unredeemable.

How can time not be unredeemable? With each changing season we hasten on toward the end of whatever time permits. "Seasons change with the scenery; weaving time in a tapestry." The line is from "A Hazy Shade of Winter," a song by the poet-songwriter Paul Simon that opens with an archetypal lament: "Time, Time, Time / See what's become of me / While I looked around / For my possibilities." The changing of the seasons was enough to hold mortals enthralled, thought poet–insurance executive Wallace Stevens. He urged

the nameless woman in "Sunday Morning" — who sat in her
peignoir in a sunny chair contemplating the feeling that she
should be in church on this Sunday morning, thinking about
the sacrifice of Jesus — to remember "the bough of summer
and the winter branch." A voice cries out to her at the end
of the poem — after she struggles to choose between reflecting on time past and Christ's sacrifice, and reflecting on the
present with its "pungent oranges" and "green freedom of a
cockatoo" — telling her: "The tomb in Palestine/Is not the
porch of spirits lingering./It is the grave of Jesus, where he
lay." Ultimately, Stevens, one of America's greatest and most
sensual, melodic, and aesthetic poets, is able to come to the
philosophical conclusion that "death is the mother of beauty."
But at the risk of sounding like a solipsist as well as an agnostic, I think, until I can establish otherwise, death is the end
of time, and time, despite having been seen for centuries as a
father, is the mother of suffering.

Chapter 12

ESCAPING TIME

Indulging in my meditations, I realize, is possible because I am privileged to live in a time and place where I am not required to engage in daily fights for food or shelter, or to face the war and pestilence and poverty that much of the human population confronts each day. My thoughts seem indulgent to me, a result of too much reading and of being what I used to jokingly call overeducated, of being too cerebral and given to what sometimes can wickedly feel like intellectual masturbation.

But am I not raising essential questions for those who do not have the comfort of belief? I can almost hear the voice of what Eric Hoffer called the true believer, the religious true believer, reverberating in my head — telling me to feel thankful for the bounty I have been given, the good fortune of living in a free country and having loved ones, good friends, good health, and work that pleases me. I should realize, says the hectoring religious true believer's voice, that my debt is to God, that my gratitude should be expressed in faith and the recognition that all I possess I owe to the grace of the one and only heavenly creator, the king of the cosmos, or as Ferlinghetti wrote in the poem, "Sometimes during Eternity," when describing the effect of Jesus on believers: "the king cat / Who's got to blow / or they can't quite make it." Would that same believer hector those without good fortune for being unworthy of God's generosity? I do not resist belief out of irreligiousness or stubbornness. I resist simply because I cannot not resist.

I did, for the most part, resist the lure of substances, however. Alcohol and other drugs can temporarily release us from time's clutches, induce feelings of euphoria, altered states of consciousness, or an invigorating spiritual potency. That was what drug use in the sixties was mostly about. If you remember the sixties, you didn't live through them, some people like to say. I was never personally drawn to consciousness-expanding drugs in that era, though much of the stretching of consciousness associated with drug use then, and now, links, I believe, to the desire to pierce the veil of consciousness and discover another reality, to find what is tantamount to higher spiritual truth and escape the albatross of time. Though, sure, lots of young people just wanted to get wasted, as many do today.

But Aldous Huxley, the celebrated novelist grandson of agnostic T. H. Huxley, advocated drug use as a way to enter the portals of higher consciousness. With mescaline, Huxley believed he saw golden lights dancing and books flowing like rubies. He also experienced what he described as a complete indifference to time, and the feeling that space had lost its predominance over his state of being. Under both mescaline and LSD, he had illuminating glimpses of the ubiquity of love and saw that one can never love enough.

Ecstasy, or MDMA, a recreational drug used in more recent years and the drug of choice for raves, creates in many of those who experiment with it a sense of timelessness and bountiful love. Carlos Castaneda, a popular figure in the sixties and seventies who gave us the Yaqui shaman Don Juan, wrote of another gateway to alternative consciousness, the use of peyote, a drug long used by Native Americans and the subject of court battles over whether it should be deemed a part of religious practice, like the communion wafer. Rastafarian spirituality is built around marijuana, or ganja. Marijuana is also connected to alternative consciousness and the spiritual practice associated with a famous American commune founded by Stephen Gaskin, whose philosophy links cannabis to spiritual sacrament and the belief that God is inside us all. William James, the father of pragmatism, who gave us *The Varieties of Religious Experience*, believed nitrous oxide stimulated mystical consciousness to an extraordinary degree.

I used to enjoy talking on the radio with the psychedelic pied piper Terence McKenna. He was a man of true brilliance (a word I try to use sparingly), an ethnobotanist, a lay scholar — a lay theologian, really — and a seeker of higher consciousness who, despite being a formidable expert on plants and James Joyce, was probably best known for his advocacy of psychedelics and their connection to religious experience. He and his brother, Dennis, traveled to the Colombian Amazon in search of higher consciousness through the use of ayahuasca, a hallucinogen described in works by William Burroughs and Allen Ginsberg. The shamanistic pursuits of the brothers McKenna led to a book called *Invisible Landscape*. Terence saw elves and space aliens and his Celtic ancestors and other spirits, and he believed at one point that he was hearing a telephone conversation his mother had had decades before.

But it was religious experience he was really seeking, and he was convinced he had combined Logos with a visionary experience fueled by psychedelic mushrooms and other psychedelic plants. When he was dying of brain cancer, Terence saw Blakean eternal light.

Drugs continue to greatly influence many who believe they are discovering another level of consciousness that is spiritual or of a surrogate spiritual nature. The drugs — including the plants and mushrooms often deemed holy — are seen as catalysts to higher truths or as paths to spiritual enlightenment, often, I suspect, because they create the illusion that the user is not bound by time. I think those who believe or want to believe they can enter another dimension by taking drugs — or by channeling spirits or seeking psychic readings or having out-of-body experiences or otherwise moving beyond what Wallace Stevens in "Sunday Morning" called "this earthly paradise" — have put their faith in a higher power. Or they are allowing themselves to believe that a spiritual ascent, a ladder into another dimension or another range of consciousness or feeling beyond the temporal, is available to them. In other words, a religious experience — one that can subdue doubt and open the mind to a different kind of light and the liberating feeling of being beyond the confinement of time as they normally experience it.

The search for such an encounter can take extreme forms, even without substances, as we saw in 1997, when thirty-eight devotees of a cult in San Diego calling themselves Heaven's Gate committed suicide in order to leave their bodies and ascend to what they believed was a higher level — specifically a spaceship the cult presumed was situated behind the comet Hale-Bopp, waiting to take them aboard. The Hale-Bopp suicides were an extraordinary example of the desire to reach a higher realm, coupled with faith in the ability to transcend the physical body, and, alas, were motivated in part by the pervasive and popular sci-fi culture.

To some, leaving the body by means of a religious or mystical experience is the ultimate way to defeat time, the annihilator. The Russian mystic Georges Gurdjieff, who strongly influenced writers Katherine Mansfield and Jean Toomer and poet Hart Crane, taught a philosophy based on the unity of the body with mind and spirit that would lead to "a birth above the body" and a spirit set free from time's shackles. The search for a higher or expanded consciousness is often a quest to release the mind from time's weight or the weight of the body and its appetites, what the poet Delmore Schwartz called "the heavy body who goes with me....A stupid clown of the spirit's motive." Think of experiencing time and consciousness in the mind alone! A number of years ago a man jumped off the Golden Gate Bridge in a suicide attempt that left everything paralyzed but his mind. As one friend of mine aptly described it, the man who jumped managed to kill everything but the one thing he wanted to kill. Some Eastern practices seek to free the mind of body consciousness, and Eastern thinking often posits that resistance comes from seeing time as linear, or from the ego and mind trapped in time. Letting go of ego and mind in order to merge with higher consciousness is what Buddhists would have us believe in — rather than the necessity of finding God. Release from ego and what Buddhists view as the mind's mirages means a release from time's flux.

Vedantic thought has had immense influence on spiritual thinking in the West. The principal idea, rooted in the Upanishads, is that life is wed to a loving morality and an immanent or transcendent force — traditionally called the Brahmin or identified in terms of cosmic consciousness — that can be reached through meditation and detachment from ego. In Buddhist thought the concept even extends to the extinction of ego — which is really what is meant by nirvana — the extinction of illusory time as we experience it, and unity with real and infinite time. Many Eastern practices, like yoga, especially meditation practices, are designed to diminish not only illusory thought attached to ego but also the burden of time that accompanies ego.

Swamis and yoga classes and spiritual teachers like Jack Kornfield have introduced much Eastern philosophy to the West. Spiritual ideas imported from the East are now nearly commonplace and are weighed down, and watered down, by Western ways. I remember thinking how metaphorical it was that a wealthy Beverly Hills matron I met at Esalen, the wife of a major Hollywood producer, was committed to teaching children yoga in schools throughout the United States. Originally from Brooklyn, and still possessing a distinct accent, she told me she had run into fundamentalist Christian parents in Iowa and Nebraska who had deep objections to their children learning or practicing yoga.

Esalen Institute, where most forms of Eastern philosophy are taught, was cofounded by Michael Murphy as a place for human transformation and secular spiritual practice. Murphy's guru was the yogi Sri Aurobindo, who was part of the freedom movement in India. Sri Aurobindo sought to combine Eastern and Western thinking by being in the world and working to bring evolution to Vedantic thought instead of viewing the world as maya, or illusion. He believed, as did both Nietzsche and George Bernard Shaw to some degree, in a higher — or in his view, divine — level of evolution and in a divine mother.

Sometimes it seems that the real, major change in America

regarding Eastern thinking and spiritual practices occurred when the Beatles became enamored of transcendental meditation and Maharishi Mahesh Yogi. Attempts to combine Eastern spiritual thought with Western traditions long preceded John, George, Paul, and Ringo, though the Beatles brought Eastern spiritual practice out into the domain of popular culture and to a different level of acceptance. John Lennon caused an uproar over a remark he made about their being "bigger than Jesus." Was the outrage because people thought Lennon was, by extension, elevating Eastern philosophy and Eastern meditative practice to a rung above Christianity? Or did they simply abhor what seemed to be the glorification of fame in the remark?

I recall a sales rep for transcendental meditation repeatedly telling me that the practice would lead me to "charming levels of consciousness." What those charming levels were I never found out, because the agnostic in me balked at the idea of transcendence for sale, despite my longing to find out if I could reach a transcendent plane. It seemed bogus to have to pay for a Colonel Sanders–style, spiritual fast food that would supply a quick route to merely a taste of satori. My rejection is not meant to diminish the scientifically proven benefits of meditation. They are real. It is simply that doubt wins out where harnessing my ego is concerned. I am as agnostic about transcendent metaphysics from the East as I am about religion- and faith-based spiritual ideas rooted in the West. None of these can necessarily help those of us who claim to be agnostic vanquish or transcend the temporal battles and mysteries of time. Think honestly about what or who allows you to temporarily escape the onus of time, and you will have discovered a great deal about who you are and what you need in this life and, if you believe in it, the next.

There have been many attempts not only to combine
Eastern and Western religious thought and practice but also
to unite the materialism and ego-centered ways of the West
with Eastern religions' spirituality and detachment from the
ego. One of Kipling's most famous lines, from "The Ballad
of East and West," is "East is east, and west is west, and never
the twain shall meet." That used to summarize what I thought
was the mutual exclusiveness of two different traditions and
paths. In Kipling's poem the twain ultimately met on the bat-
tlefield, and throughout the years the twain have met under
more auspicious circumstances. Emerson's transcendentalism
and his notion of an Oversoul link East and West, as does, for
that matter, Whitman's cosmic consciousness. Popular American culture is replete with watered-down versions of East
meets West, especially in the world of the still-extant Human
Potential Movement.

Nevertheless, Western thinking is linear and features an
eschatology that sees time moving along a linear trajectory.
Womb to tomb. Life to death to afterlife. In the case of Jesus,
life to death to resurrection. Eastern thinking, in contrast, is
rooted in *kalpas* and *pralayas*. Time is cyclical. The one major
Western exception to that division, interestingly enough, was
the medieval Cathars, French heretics who, by most historical accounts, catalyzed the Roman Catholic–led Inquisition
of the twelfth century. The Cathars believed in reincarnation,
rejected oaths and marriage, and viewed the God of the Old
Testament as the devil or as a less important deity than the
higher, supreme God. Most of them were murdered.

In the sixties I saw parochial-school-trained Catholics,
synagogue-reared Jews, and Protestants of all denominations
turn to the ideology of the left and what we called the Movement, the political, collective pipe dream of that era, and its

liberation theology. And then, years later in Northern California, I observed Michael Murphy, who had turned to Eastern religions and the Human Potential Movement. After the Beatles brought the Maharishi into the world spotlight, a swarm of swamis followed into the United States, including Osho (Bhagwan Shree Rajneesh), the chubby little guru infamous for a personal fleet of Rolls Royces who inspired a self-contained would-be utopian community in Oregon. This community proved toxic and corrupt, but it was based on the premise that Western materialism and Eastern spiritual practice could be melded.

Can we, especially in the West, really detach from ego and the material world? When I think of detachment from ego and from the allegedly illusory material world, I think of how elevating self-enrichment and self-enhancement and self-esteem can be for me, and how easily my mood can shift to one of enjoyment of luxury or even hedonistic or sybaritic pleasures without feeling time. I think, too, in a more serious vein, of the often quoted words of the Jewish sage Hillel, possibly a contemporary of Moses, who said, "If I am not for myself, who will be? And if not for myself, what am I? And if not now, when?" Hillel believed in the law as specified in the Torah, in loving peace and in not doing to another what was hateful to oneself. But self was inseparable from his ethos. How can I not be for myself?

So much Western thought is rooted in Cartesian thinking, including a simple, unadorned statement by Descartes, "Cogito ergo sum." I think therefore I am. (Or as my old friend Herb Gold put it when writing about *Waiting for Godot*: "I stink therefore I am.") The Cartesian emphasis is on the first person singular. I exist because I think and because I am me and no one else. Yet as Christopher Lasch and a battalion of

head doctors and self-appointed cultural critics have made
abundantly clear, the West, particularly the United States, has
seen so much emphasis on self that the culture has become one
of narcissism. Narcissism is, in fact, supposed to be largely a
Western affliction, though the word has been diluted by over-
use and lost much of its original clinical meaning. Can self-
absorption or self-obsessiveness be extinguished by donning
saffron robes and sitting contemplatively in Himalayan caves,
or by meditating with pure, ascetic intent? Is it wrong to be
self-involved or taken in by material glitter? Eastern thinking
and its spiritual practices have a great deal to do with reaching
points of stillness, with moving beyond the world of objects
and into the oneness of self that rests in immateriality beyond
time.

Chapter 13

DELIVER US FROM EVIL

*I*f evil abides and flourishes, how are we to live in peace? The Lord's Prayer asks of the heavenly father that we transgressive mortals collectively not be led into temptation, and that we be delivered from evil. Oscar Wilde memorably (and aphoristically, and probably flippantly) said that the only way to get rid of temptation is to yield to it. The evil I wanted to avoid in my evolving code of personal conduct was not necessarily the evil that came from temptation. There was, I knew, aggression and cruelty in me, my own heart of darkness. Could it not serve me? Were not my devils, as Rilke poignantly said of his art, also my angels?

In high school I was considered by some to be a big mouth and an obnoxious kid because I put into words, without censoring myself, whatever leaped to mind. It didn't matter if the words were hurtful, so long as they were honest or amused me or my cronies. I liked to think of myself as a likable kid, but it was clear that many did not like me and a few even shunned me. So, as a high school senior I re-created myself, as I had in elementary school when I was getting beaten up by my sixth grade teacher for acting up or speaking out of turn in class. I could make myself good, I had realized as an eleven-year-old, instead of acting up. I could win the approval of my classmates and my teacher by acting the role of the good boy. I wanted, in the sixth grade and then again in high school, to feel liked, because in both instances I had made myself unlikable, which made me unhappy. Good or bad seemed in large part to be a willful choice.

Being a sometimes cruel and abrasive loudmouth in high school had not endeared me to many of my peers, and had made me disliked in ways that were easy for an insecure boy to internalize. But I hardly qualified as a signifier of evil, and I worked at changing myself. As for evil, I realized early on with a child's awareness that there was evil in the form of violence and aggression outside of what was inside of me. The most extreme example I knew of was the Shoah, but I knew of it without really comprehending the breadth and scope of the persecution and exterminations until I learned more about it. I saw *War of the Worlds* as a kid and was mesmerized by the priest in the film walking toward the Martians, scary as hell by the standards of the day, reciting the twenty-third psalm: "I fear no evil / for thou art with me." God was there to protect me should I find myself, like the priest, walking in the valley of the shadow of death or confronted, God forbid, by Jew-killing Nazis or some other manifestation of evil.

I studied *Julius Caesar* in junior high and liked the sound of Brutus's words about the evil men do living after them. But evil was still at best an elusive concept, a notion attached to a mythical character with horns and a pitchfork who preferred to reside in a place that would never freeze over and likely did not exist. As I grew older and into agnostic thinking, I recognized evil in the multiple nightmares of history, the corruption and victimization of children, hurtful bigotry, malice, dehumanizing racism, cruelty, oppression, and wanton, indiscriminate violence. Evil was, it seemed, a force field with its own nature and its own magnetic lure. As an adult, I also saw evil in the kidnappings by sexual predators and the murders of children. Was there any more appropriate signifier?

As a boy I had been fascinated by some of the tough guys, greasers we called them back then, who seemed to relish violence for its own sake, which in some cases crossed the line into what I began to think of as evil — as when a delinquent kicked my neighbor Slimy Hymie in the balls because Slimy didn't have a match for the delinquent's cigarette. Then there was Tony the Crutch, a paraplegic who would swing his steel crutch at the groin of an unsuspecting passerby and shout "score" if he hit his gonad target. My neighbor Froggy was badly beaten by a carful of greasers out cruising for a random victim. Gratuitous violence, it seemed, could strike anyone at any time. I became friendly with some of the greasers, and some were pretty bad boys — not quite the romanticized greaser we would see Henry Winkler portray as the Fonz in *Happy Days*. But were they evil?

One afternoon at Cain Park, where many of us hung out as teens during the summer, a pack of girls chased another girl and beat her. A clean-cut, good-guy football player named Mickey stopped the violence by standing in the way of the aggressors so the girl getting beaten up could escape. Mickey told the girls he didn't want to see one person being picked on. The girls screamed profanities at him and swore they would get their boyfriends to come to the park for payback. As bad luck would have it, I was on my way out of the park with a guy we called Fatboy Howie when a cadre of evil-looking hoods, none of whom I had ever seen before, entered with baseball bats and chains and cornered us. I counted nine of them. Fatboy and I had unwittingly walked into imminent serious violence. We were trapped. It didn't matter that the girls had filled these greasers with lies about their being beaten up by Mickey, and it didn't matter that we weren't really even friends of Mickey. They wanted, quite simply, to release their aggression.

Perhaps, like Mickey, they believed they were acting with honor. The leader of the group pointed at me with the baseball bat he was carrying, and then, saying "We're gonna take you over there," pointed to a small, isolated glenlike area about twenty or thirty yards away. "We're gonna pound your fucking heads in. But first tell me," he quickly added, "you got a brother?" My mind raced. Could he possibly know my brother, Vic, who had been a star football player? It seemed impossible, because these were guys I had never laid eyes on, but I told him Vic was my brother. Whereupon the leader grabbed my arm and the others joined in, grabbing Fatboy and me, pushing and shoving us toward the area the leader had pointed out with his bat. The leader said, "Now we're gonna beat your fuckin' heads in." This was the real deal. I knew they meant to do exactly what he said.

What happened next could be attributed to fast, intuitive thinking or just dumb luck on my part. Art S. suddenly and seemingly miraculously popped into my mind. Art was a greaser I knew only slightly from Wally's, a greaser pool hall where I would occasionally hang out despite my father's warnings against my ever even going into a pool hall. I'd been told, though it had not been for many months, that I looked like Art. I blurted out, "You thought Art S. was my brother," and I instantly knew I'd hit a bull's-eye. The greaser-in-charge, who had asked me if I had a brother, not only knew Art, but bought it when I lied and told him Art was my cousin. One of the gang looked skeptical at this, so, with what felt like a forced effort, I added, "Art is my mother's first cousin's stepson." I could tell the made-up-on-the-spot kinship — which, as they would have known, had they thought about it, meant no blood relation between me and Art — had deflated the aggression. The utterance of the magic name had saved us, or rather had saved me, since the greasers still wanted to beat up Fatboy Howie. Knowing full well that I was really pushing it, I said Fatboy Howie was my cousin, and they let us go.

How do we define evil? Genocide, war, bigotry, wanton cruelty, child molestation, murder, rape, and actions stemming from deep animus are far more apt subjects than a potential greaser head-banging to begin grappling with in any attempt to understand the nature of evil, if indeed there is such a thing as a force of evil. But the Israeli novelist Amos Oz defined evil for me as aggression. What kind of aggression? Constructive or benevolent aggression can save lives. Who or what do you see when you think of evil? I watched a television show's reconstruction of a despicable crime, in which a guy and his female companion kidnapped an elderly couple ostensibly to rob them. But the male perpetrator took both of these frail and sweet old people out to a remote area and bashed them to death with a tire iron. I call that an act of evil. In *Overcoming Speechlessness*, Alice Walker writes of Congo warriors raping a mother and her daughter and killing the father and son after trying to force the son and then the daughter to eat the leg of the mother — which they had severed with machetes and then fried. However one wishes to signify such acts, the agnostic in me also asks the fundamental and unanswerable question of why they occur. Why are they part of what some insist on calling the grand scheme?

Is evil palpable? I think so. Think of child killers or those who otherwise harm people without cause or for the most foolish or ignorant of reasons. After 9-11, a man in Arizona murdered a Sikh because he was wearing a turban and the killer identified him with Osama bin Laden. I have been touched by the goodness of people, but evil touches too. It seems to be a force we come up against, and one that can also reside in our own hearts, even in a banal heart, as the philosopher Hannah Arendt pointed out in her essay on the Nazi murderer Adolf Eichmann. We talk of wanting to see or bring out the good in someone, or of bringing out the worst, and we often hear the cliché about the good and bad in all of us. Yet there are people who are as toxic as rattlers, full of what Coleridge called "motiveless malignity," a phrase that aptly describes Iago's actions in making evil his good in *Othello*, and Satan's actions in Milton's *Paradise Lost*.

The phrase *motiveless malignity* makes me think, too, of Claggart in Melville's *Billy Budd*. Billy's innocence, and something indeterminate in Claggart that hated this innocence, brought forth from the ship's master-at-arms an irrational need to destroy Billy. Melville and Shakespeare provide no answers, because they could brilliantly depict evil but, despite their genius, understood it no better than we agnostics understand why we are here and whether there is a force behind our existence. What force, hidden or otherwise, lies behind evil? The destructive impulse in humans was a cultural meme in Nazi Germany, a force that raged against blacks in the days of Jim Crow and lynchings in the American South, and a force the Turks used against Armenians, and the Congolese used against their own. It took murderous hold in Cambodia,

Rwanda, Bosnia, and Darfur, and it led to the murder of thousands on 9-11. It removes from the human heart any possibility of seeing or caring about the humanity of the other.

If one acknowledges evil as a force, one must ask where it comes from and why it exists. Is it, perhaps, simply a part of what we call nature, including human nature? I remember an intense discussion I had with the novelist Joyce Carol Oates, in which she seemed persuaded that acts of evil have their etiology, that they are inevitably the effects of specific causes. People hate and oppress others, said Oates, because they have themselves been maltreated, or for other reasons whose causes can be determined. I found myself arguing with her, insisting that the reason or cause behind what we deem evil can, in some instances, be indeterminate, even nonexistent.

One sees dualism, the binary of good and evil, or of construction versus destruction, in much theology and intellectual hypothesizing. How do we reconcile these two seemingly antithetical forces when they can and often do bleed into each other? How do we begin to understand the complexity of human nature, which is as mysterious as God and the cosmos? The influential Manichaean heresy posed a division between good and evil with the outcome yet to be determined. Manichaeanism also saw a split between body and soul and between the material and the spiritual. Such binaries are pervasive in Western thinking and are the basis of post-structuralist and deconstructionist thought and are often intertwined, as is evident in the Eastern concept of yin and yang. Can binaries be synthesized? Need they be? Or are binaries simply a constant? If one believes in good and evil, is it possible to have one without the other?

Consider for a moment, in the context of binaries, the hyphenated identity of the *African American*, a term less common

than the preferred *black* or *person of color* but nevertheless indicative of an inherent split between ancestral heritage and
the American world. For all ethnicities in America, there has
been an ongoing philosophical split between identities past
and present; and for African Americans the split took shape
early, in the dichotomy between the ideas of Booker T. Washington, which emphasized the masses and jobs and separation, and those of W. E. B. DuBois, which emphasized the
so-called talented tenth and culture and amalgamation. A similar dichotomy faced director Spike Lee when he came to the
end of his film *Do the Right Thing*. Is it the right thing to
follow the pacific-civil-disobedience and turn-the-other-cheek
precepts of Martin Luther King, or to engage in by-any-means-
necessary actions, which may include busting the storefront
window, an idea attached to the philosophy of Malcolm X?

Such binaries may have to be viewed case by case. But one
of the challenges in establishing a viable personal moral code
is to understand the complexity of binaries and come to a reli-
able synthesis — if synthesis is possible! Good and evil seem
to be binaries, but the road to hell, we know, is paved with
good intentions; and the good is, as Brutus said, often interred
with the bones, while the evil endures. Good and evil are
often hopelessly intertwined. Oscar Schindler thought Jews
were similar to dogs — they were cheap, exploitable labor —
but he courageously placed himself in great danger and saved
Jewish lives. Many notions have been posited in an attempt to
make sense out of such binaries. Evil thinking versus virtuous
good action in the same man, as in Schindler's case? The heart
against itself? The complexity of the human will? Bifurcated
man? Thomas Jefferson, a slave owner, gave us the Declaration of Independence. And before the Civil War and his issu-
ance of the Emancipation Proclamation, Lincoln, without any

apparent moral pangs, wanted to send all blacks off to colonize Liberia.

But let me return to evil qua evil. If I build a code, is everything in it permissible, even whatever I determine to be evil, or think of as evil? What will give it moral force, and how am I to decide the nature of evil, and how and when to shun or battle it? But perhaps most important, can living by the notion "Don't be evil," which the visionary leaders of world-famous Google have taken as the company's ruling philosophy, bring peace? Who is to say who or what is evil? If, as Google has done, you build a code that includes a clause against doing evil, what does it mean? Your code may be no less valid than the code of any organized religion, but of course there is no one to offer guidance if you stray from your principles or don't know how to apply them.

If I should ignore my code and choose evil, there will be no priest to absolve me with an assigned number of Hail Mary's. No minister of God will instruct me in finding a redemptive path, no imam will assure me of the way back to the path to paradise, no rabbi will enlighten me on the ways of the Lord who led my people — notwithstanding the Khazars — out of Egypt. I will be alone, waiting for that mustard seed of faith that I doubt I will find, or the wisdom I hope will come to me so I can understand the nature of evil and why I must set myself against it.

If my code is to live for the pleasure of the moment, am I being selfish or, worse, hedonistic, possibly even evil? If I act selflessly am I sacrificing self, giving up potential bounty, which could be a kind of evil against myself and my interests — even though brain scans reveal that some people derive great satisfaction from acting altruistically? Questions such as these poked at me as I began to establish a life for myself as a

professor and scholar and then as a journalist and public figure. I avoided, as best I could, committing the trespasses that
bordered on personal evil, but I wondered, and on occasion
stewed and even agonized over, whether I was doing enough
to fight the evil that riddled the moral landscape.

I identified as a personal weakness the fact that I liked people to like me. I liked approval. That was a strength too, since
it allowed me to reap social capital and enhanced my self-
esteem. But it often prompted me to do the wrong thing for con-
formity's sake or approval, to dress myself in ways that suited
others more than myself. Approval was the primary reason I
joined a fraternity in college and went through the stupid and
demeaning pledge process and even more idiotic initiation,
what was called hell week and hell night, names that seemed to
mock evil. Looking for God and for a hidden force greater than
myself to justify my personal morality also seemed a weakness to me. Should we not have the courage to hobble through
life and make decisions about good and evil without the crutch
of the divine, since we are, after all, alone?

I succeeded in getting people to like me by respecting others and trying to bring out the best in myself and in them, and
by not caving in to my censor-free, aggressive impulses. I was
fortunate enough to be curious about other people and to be
by nature a good listener and a man of warmth and humor. I
wanted to establish a good name for myself, and I was suc-
ceeding. But I also wondered if this didn't mean I was giving
up myself for the sake of others' good opinion. Did I need to
put others' opinions ahead of mine? I had become, it seemed
to me, too sensitive to the good opinion of others! I needed to
think of all the great men and women, even the most revered
and beloved, who stirred up enmity by fighting evil and doing
what they believed was right, good, or true. Think of Thoreau

and Gandhi. Raoul Wallenberg. Martin Luther King Jr. Harriet Tubman. Rosa Parks. Margaret Sanger. Hannah Senesh. Or of all the heroic men and women whose names are not known or written in our history books.

Who was important enough to seek approbation from? Should I seek goodwill indiscriminately? And why should the goodwill of others matter? Is goodwill really good or good for us? Wasn't my inner approbation what mattered? These were the questions of a young man in the process of building a life's resume more substantial than the one that would have merited only a sentence or two in an obituary had I died on that Ohio highway. But the same or similar questions persisted as the years flew by. As I moved on to teaching and to National Public Radio, to the life I would carve out for myself in Northern California, T. S. Eliot still influenced me. How could I be certain of anything, including the nature of good and evil, without his kind of certainty?

What could possibly be more important than finding a way out of nothingness, and a firm, lasting reason for rejecting evil? Those were far more important than being liked, or as Arthur Miller's Willy Loman would have it, being well liked. Wasn't rejection of evil at the core of all the great religions? Didn't one need to find a way to know evil even in a world where defining evil as an absolute can be nearly impossible, especially since I neither saw nor heard God? Where good and evil were concerned, did I really have to wait for a sacred or metaphysical presence to enlighten me? Shouldn't I be obliged to find my own threads of goodness and pull them together?

Robert Frost's sonnet "Design," first published in 1922, gives us a view of transcendent power that changes the equation of the once-everlasting God and evil into a far more frightening calculus:

I found a dimpled spider, fat and white
On a white heal-all, holding up a moth
Like a white piece of rigid satin cloth —
Assorted characters of death and blight
Mixed ready to begin the morning right,
Like the ingredients of a witches' broth —
A snow-drop spider, a flower like a froth,
And dead wings carried like a paper kite.

What had that flower to do with being white,
The wayside blue and innocent heal-all?
What brought the kindred spider to that height,
Then steered the white moth thither in the night?
What but design of darkness to appall? —
If design govern in a thing so small.

In this poem, Frost, a poet of the binaries of fire and ice
who is usually identified with swinging birch trees and walks
in the woods on snowy nights, presents a black mass, a micro-
cosmic execution of innocence. As Randall Jarrell and others
have pointed out, it seems conclusive in the poem that a divine hand is behind the killing portrayed in the poem's first
stanza — until we arrive at the question posed at the poem's
end. That question presents another possibility. What appears
to be a design of darkness, a slaughtering of innocence in
which the master designer must be complicit, might just turn
out to be not an orchestrated design at all but a design to appall that comes out of chaos and randomness.

We appear to be in a dark period of world terror. It is different, to be sure, from the darkness of Nazism that fell over
the continent with Hitler's rise to power, which began a few
years before Frost published his sonnet. And it is different from
the cold war that soon followed the defeat of the Axis powers.

The cold war had to do in part with the deep and abiding religious faith of Americans set against what came to be seen as evil, godless communism. Remember the parodic-sounding rallying cry during the Vietnam War: "Kill a commie for Christ"? There was, of course, much more to the cold war than Western religious faith versus Bolshevik atheism, but the major underlying factor was distrust and hostility between the United States and the Soviet Union, rooted in irreconcilable belief systems — individualism versus collectivism — and the perception of each that the other was evil. Should Americans have had more respect and tolerance for the Soviets and their strong view that religion was an opiate of the people? And should Americans now accept the Islamic warriors who believe their religion is the only way, the sole path for humankind?

The right to believe ought to be inviolable, and disallowing others' beliefs ought to be considered a form of evil. The Russians or Islamic warriors can, of course, believe any idea they please, but both have done, and continue to do, evil in the name of those beliefs. With rising nationalism and oil wealth in Russia, and the seemingly relentless rise of Islamic fundamentalist fervor and the Arab oil wealth that fuels it, there are now legitimate concerns about evil attempts by the Russians, with their vestiges of postcommunism, and by the extreme Islamists, with their longing to shift global hegemonies, to impose their beliefs on others. And yes, much evil has been done in the name of democracy and nearly every brand of militant nationalism.

Before glasnost and perestroika and the fall of what Ronald Reagan called the evil empire, the Soviets were living under an oppressive system that had set itself up to follow a script of eventual global hegemony. The threat to Americans was that

the Soviets would try to impose their belief in the state, and
in its eventual withering away, on us and stamp out our belief
in individual liberty and God. All the lawsuits and the carrying on about separation of church and state notwithstanding,
America was and is, in the eyes of most of its citizens, one
nation under God. American capitalism and moneygrubbing
and economic control of the many by the few, as well as the
few's ownership and control of the means of production and
distribution, were anathema to the Soviets, despite their own
ruling class of communists. The Soviets saw the United States
as the imperialistic hegemon; and in the United States, the
ruling class and others saw Soviet collectivism and the state
takeover of private enterprise as heretical and evil. The two
countries inevitably devised a system of mutually assured destruction that kept the nuclear genie in the bottle, but did not
keep believers on each side from seeing the opposite as evil.

Now, in our post-9-11 world, Islamic fanatics have demonized America, and they have replaced Kremlin acolytes
as the enemy seeking global hegemony by any means necessary. Even a parodic figure like Mike Meyers's Dr. Evil in the
Austin Powers films reflects the perceived menace of world
domination by a nefarious source. The present threat began
with the contemporary rise of Islamic fanaticism in Iran,
when Ayatollah Khomeini declared the United States, which
had helped to set up the Peacock Throne of the shah and the
rule of the Pahlavi clan, to be the great Satan. In turn, many
in the United States have demonized all Muslims as being like
those who crashed planes into the World Trade Center and the
Pentagon or slashed off Daniel Pearl's head. The tendency to
demonize the enemy has appeared in the battle between Hutus
and Tutsis in Rwanda, between Serbs and Croats and Muslims in the former Yugoslavia, and between Jews and Arabs

throughout the Middle East. In a speech delivered at the United Nations in 2006, Venezuelan president Hugo Chavez spoke of President George W. Bush as the devil. Bush, who had described the events of 9-11 as evil, had spoken there the day before, and Chavez claimed that he could still smell the sulfur. Bush had also spoken of Iraq, Iran, and North Korea as "the axis of evil."

If my code is not to dehumanize, not to strip other human beings of their humanity by demonizing them or objectifying them in a way that makes them the enemy, the heretic, the other, then I must be able to determine who, specifically, my enemy is, or if there is an enemy, and who is potentially in alliance with evil and may dehumanize or demonize me or others. This, alas, is another matter in which God, even if one believes in theodicy, provides no help.

Chapter 14

DOING GOOD

$\mathcal{W}$hether Jesus was the son of God, a prophet, or a man, and whether he even existed, the New Testament assures us that he told humankind that the greatest commandment is to love God with all our hearts, minds, and souls. How can an agnostic love a God that the seeker cannot verify, with a soul that is unverifiable? There is, alas, no visual evidence of a soul in *Gray's Anatomy*. I feel from time to time as if I have a soul, or something resembling what I conceptualize as a soul, and it feels as if it requires some form of spiritual nourishment. Then my intellect intercedes and dismisses such notions as fantasy or as what imagination or emotion or myth brings forth without even a scintilla of proof. The idea of God, like the notion of the soul, enters and exits but never quite does more than that, even though I sometimes feel moved to discover a basis for a soul or for faith, to feel agape, the nonerotic love humans feel for God and vice versa. But while love of God may be Judeo-Christianity's highest and most sanctified ideal, how can I love what I cannot know? Jesus's commandments, delivered in his Sermon on the Mount and recorded in the New Testament — that we must love our neighbors as ourselves and love our enemies — are improbable and foolish and, for most thinking organisms, unattainable.

Why should love be so indiscriminate, so inconsequential, as to apply to all our fellow humans — including those disposed to do evil? This seems to me a promiscuous and nondiscerning love. Think of Alexander Pope's "To err is human / To forgive divine." Is forgiveness, like love, an indiscriminate virtue, to be ladled out even to those who have earned our enmity? The clerics and religious discoursers and homily makers tell us divine love is what we must strive for. They set the bar too high and urge us to achieve what many of us cannot. Instead of trying to clear an impossibly high bar, one should consider living by a personally crafted ethical code of virtue rooted in agnosticism and value tolerance up to a point.

When the God of the Old Testament killed the Egyptians who pursued the departing Hebrews, he was said to have noted that the Egyptians too were his children, and that their deaths in the Red Sea should be mourned. Even the enemy Egyptians deserved such recognition, because they were human and children of God. But God was relentless in the plagues he visited on Pharaoh and the Egyptians — even killing their firstborn — and Jesus said he had come to put the son against the father and the daughter against the mother. I don't want to slip into citing the obvious inconsistencies in the two testaments, because there are too many and they testify, so to speak, to how contradictory God, Jesus, and Moses are in what they say and do, or at least this is so if one gives credence to holy writ. How can we find the absolute in the inconsistent? We cannot. For many of us, the answer, once again, sides with agnosticism, which has no answers. The answer is that, until further notice, there is no answer.

Having no answers does not preclude seeking them, just as not believing in a soul does not preclude searching for experiences that feed what we think of as our souls. If you don't believe in the soul, think of what moves you most deeply. Does it feel like something that can be signified simply by emotion? Asking if there is or isn't a soul can sometimes seem like asking if there is or isn't God. Music can affect our moods and what we generally think of as our souls. Some of the songs of the early soul singers, such as Smokey Robinson, Aretha Franklin, and Sam Cooke, and the so-called white soul of the Righteous Brothers, stir what feels like soul in me. Are there really soul mates?

What feels like the soul in me occasionally feels as if it rises to a higher level of being. I felt elevated when I gave a short speech to fifteen hundred sworn-in naturalized U.S. citizens. I was moved by the ceremony and ritual, just as I had been at commencements where I have delivered speeches: I felt lifted toward what seemed like a higher plane. I felt elevated, too, when I marched in cap and gown to "Pomp and Circumstance," and when my children did. I felt strongly stirred when I stood, with thousands of others, with my hand over my heart and sang "The Star-Spangled Banner" before a baseball game. I feel elevated when I read a great and (unavoidable signifier ahead!) soul-stirring work of literature or view an extraordinary painting or sculpture or hear music that moves through me, quickening and heightening my emotions. Is it my soul that is affected? It certainly feels like something deeper, more profound, than the word *emotion* can convey. I like to savor that feeling, which, like anything in life worth savoring, is much too fleeting.

The ephemeral stirrings that make life worth living are not worth dying over. But I wonder, are such elevated, call them soulful, responses tied to a wellspring of spiritual hunger? The kinds of activities I write of here are hardly sacred or capable of elevating me to anything beyond the quotidian — as opposed to a higher realm of consciousness that comes close to what traditionally has been called God. Or are they? Is watching a gorgeous sunset, or seeing deer on a mountain, or looking in awe at the heavenly constellations, or seeing resplendent flowers blooming, or watching a cheetah racing gracefully not a way of feeling elevation that approaches what at least seems like a higher source? William James wrote about our solemnity and enthusiasms in connection with religious experience, and about our "wild zest." He called it a gift, our search for moments that lift us from unhappiness and the essential despair of the human condition. But belief, James also pointed out, is not rational.

So I'm back to a central question. If no spiritual power is visible behind life's elevations, or behind the Ten Commandments or scripture…and if we doubt the origins of moral or spiritual authority…and if we cannot determine what is worth dying for…and if we are as uncertain whether the soul exists…then how do we derive purpose, our code, our meaning? The answer appears to be: from whatever sources we choose.

As the Bible's importance — the word of a God I could not fathom — began to wane for me, I tried to see Godlike power in art, particularly literary art. The artist, like God, creates a world and then removes himself or herself from it for the rest of time, though it remains a creation within the creation for others to interpret and be affected by. This kind of Deism — connecting God to creation but removing him from involvement in it — is at the heart of the spiritual thinking of individuals like Voltaire and Thomas Jefferson. When I failed at becoming an artist, it was a failure of my imagination, but it felt like a failure to ascend to the higher plane of art. If I could truly have seen art as a creator of art, I might have had a good replacement for God. Aesthetics and the worship of art can provide a surrogate, just as a belief in nature or Marxism, or just about anything, can. But if there is no replacement for the eternal, one must continue to wait.

One can wait without answers and still choose to fill the allotted time with good deeds. One can seek to do good prompted by nothing more than the elevated and soulful feelings that such acts bring, or because one simply believes that doing good is the right thing to do. We speak of practical-minded people as being grounded, as having their feet firmly planted on the ground, while many spiritual seekers and spiritual finders are seen as airheaded, flighty. One can, of course, be both practical and spiritual. Yet I am continually surprised, and often uplifted and amazed, by those who give up self and seek spiritual fulfillment in attending the needs of others. Many, like my old friend Ram Dass, are what I call truly spiritual. Born Richard Alpert, he wrote *Be Here Now* and, with Timothy Leary, pioneered LSD experimentation. I don't know whether he believes in a higher power, but both before and after a stroke terribly debilitated him, this spiritual teacher has epitomized much about compassion and service in the work he would eventually do while caring for the dying.

Can agnostics engage in the nobler service of others, without a spiritual platform and without the drive to do good deeds that is often part of a spiritual philosophy or predicated on a spiritual doctrine or on a commandment to love? Of course. The hedonist mantra (an oxymoron?) "If it feels good, do it" can apply to feeling good about doing good and to seeking fulfillment apart from ego or material gratification. Doing good because it feels good is simple and practical and far less serious-minded than doing good because God wills it, or because one hopes to find a halo in the afterlife, or even because it feeds the spiritual soul.

I remember thinking, as a Boy Scout, that doing good deeds like helping old ladies cross the street might lead to a merit badge, but also that doing such deeds simply felt good. In fact, as I got older I found that the best feelings came from doing good deeds automatically, without premeditation or self-congratulation. Tolstoy said it pretty well, even if he overstated it: "Joy can be real only if people look on their life as service, and have a definite object in life outside themselves and their personal happiness."

In my years as a broadcast journalist, fulfilling a mission (a word identified with religious work) of public service, I have been moved by displays of selflessness by many of those I interviewed. I've been moved by the patience and forbearance of youth counselors and teachers of special education classes. By nurses and other health professionals who care for the elderly and the homeless, and who dedicate themselves to what is commonly called God's work. By hospice workers who sit beside the dying and help them out of life, with the aim of allowing them a dignified end. By relief workers who aided the victims of Hurricane Katrina. By Harvard psychiatrist Jim Gordon, who went to New Orleans to help those suffering from depression after Katrina, and who went for the same purpose to Bosnia and Gaza and Israel. By the famous hairdresser Vidal Sassoon, who raised money for, and gave a good sum of his own to, Habitat for Humanity after seeing the devastation from Katrina. By former president Jimmy Carter, who voluntarily built houses for Habitat for Humanity, personally

brokered peace, and monitored elections. By the teams of doctors and health care and relief workers who went to Haiti after
the devastating earthquake there. By Greg Mortenson, who,
ignoring mortal threats and great personal danger, helped
build schools in rural Pakistan and Afghanistan.

I interviewed physicians from Doctors without Borders
and human rights activists who went to the underdeveloped
world to work on the front lines and in the trenches with sur-
vivors of mass slaughter and the horrors of war. I shook hands
with award-winning workers of the International Rescue Committee and with veterans who came back to the United States
with physical and psychic wounds after serving their country.
I talked with Oakland grandmothers who cared for the crack-
addicted babies of their addicted children, and with Israelis and
Palestinians who were passionately working together to lessen
tensions and hasten the all-too-dim possibility of peace in what
remains one of the world's most volatile regions, and with Crips
and Bloods who were intent on speaking with, rather than randomly shooting at, each other. I talked with Dr. Paul Farmer,
who set up clinics for AIDS victims in Haiti and for tuber-
culosis sufferers in Siberia. I spoke with volunteers who went
to help tsunami victims, and I talked on air with volunteers
who had joined VISTA or the Peace Corps or given themselves
over to environmental causes or to candidates they believed
in. Many of those who were dedicated to seemingly selfless
pursuits did what they did for a range of reasons, religious or
spiritual or personal and ego-gratifying or all of the above. But
the unifying factor appears to be a drive to do good, to help,
to heal, to repair, to give of oneself for an elevating cause or
simply for the reward of feeling good by doing good. Does
such a drive come from God? From the soul? From neurons
and DNA? Does it matter?

I like to think that I too am doing good by being an educator and public radio broadcaster, and by devoting time outside those vocational public service roles to helping a wide variety of community causes and charitable organizations. Paradoxically, I feel as if I am reducing the burden of my ego, freeing myself somewhat from the onus of time, and giving myself the feeling of doing good. I know, too, that my ego is invested in the work I do and the recognition I receive. By doing good, I get kudos and gratitude from others that bring good feelings, that make me feel I am a good guy.

Does it matter that I am not driven by faith or spirit when I give my presumably precious time to orphans, veterans, victims of domestic abuse, the homeless, the mentally ill, or children or other patients dying from incurable diseases? Or is my giving actually soul based? Does my ego's strong involvement diminish the value of my service? Is the service of those responding to a higher calling more valuable? Think about what good you do and why you feel compelled to do it. Determining the difference between self-enhancement and altruism can be challenging, vexing.

If I have neither the temperament nor the DNA to help build houses for the poor or care for the sick, and would rather give my time and energy to other missions and worthy causes, can I still consider myself good for doing what I feel better able to do? Is there a hierarchy of good deeds unrelated to God or faith or spirituality or, for that matter, the superego? Does one literally give up self when doing something selfless? Should one? The pivotal question, however, is: do I need belief in God or a soul in order to feel good about doing good, when by doing good I can diminish the crucible of time and ratchet down my sense of self, which can weigh me down?

My answer is: no. I can diminish my overriding sense of ego by giving up my self in ways that ultimately enhance my self!

Belief rests on emotions. Emotions can follow thinking and often do, but I believe (I think? I feel?) spiritual belief is wedded more to emotion or the need for it. In matters spiritual, "I think therefore I am" is often turned into "I feel therefore it is." The believer emphasizes feelings that seem to come from God or a higher spiritual source. The agnostic feels occasional yearning for those feelings without being able to name or know the source. Either way, one can choose to do good. One can live while waiting to die by promoting a higher good and doing good deeds that bring one up to a higher plane.

Did those devastated by Katrina, I wonder, who saw its rampaging power to destroy life and property, believe they were watching God? *Their Eyes Were Watching God* is Zora Neale Hurston's moving story about the initiation of a young black girl named Janie into life and love. The book derives its title from the devastating power of the hurricane that occurs in Florida in the novel. Are killer hurricanes God's way of being watched or seen? Are tsunamis or earthquakes or tornadoes? So-called acts of God indiscriminately kill. Robert Oppenheimer may have thought (but probably never said) those famous words from the Bhagavad Gita when he unleashed the nuclear genie: "I am become death, the destroyer of worlds." But did God create Oppenheimer so he could be the prime mover of our nuclear destruction? Nature has its destructive and lethal so-called acts of God; and men and women who, like Oppenheimer, can create death and destruction are often said to be playing God. How are we ever to reconcile our ideas about spirituality, enlightenment, and doing good with the idea of a God or transcendent force that indiscriminately and relentlessly and ruthlessly destroys or chooses to remain uninvolved, perhaps like James Joyce's notion of the artist sitting apart from it all, paring his fingernails? Can the God who commands us not to kill be a mass murderer? Is our God and the God of our fathers and mothers, the God who created us, also a destroyer of worlds? Or is he quite possibly as uninvolved as those bystanders in New York who heard Kitty Genovese screaming and pleading for help as she was stabbed to death while they remained immobile?

I would like to believe in God, to know there is spiritual power over us. But if indeed that power exists, then I am faced with accepting that it is responsible for the wanton and merciless destruction in the world and indiscriminate lethality, which makes this spiritual power seem utterly apathetic. I believe, this explains why the old God, anthropomorphic and omnipotent, involved in the human spectacle, has, for many, morphed into an aggregate of undefined, wisplike spiritual feelings and become a force like the one in *Star Wars*, or a presence-at-large within us or outside of us that can be experienced by all of us. But neither this nor the not-knowing of agnosticism translates into a reason that would prevent us from doing good.

Chapter 15

COSMIC JOKING

One day after a keynote speech to the League of Women Voters in Berkeley, I signed a number of copies of my book *Off Mike*. Later, after leaving the event, I glanced at the program, noticed the date, August 21, and realized I had autographed the books with the wrong date, August 22. The thought of God as the cosmic joker once again entered my mind uninvited as I thought morbidly to myself, what if this day, August 21, was to be my death day? There are many ways I could die suddenly, too many to catalogue. But say that, as I drove home that day, I got hit by an oncoming car, or that a stroke or cardiac arrest suddenly dealt me a fatal blow. There would be a record for years to come of my posthumous signature.

I realized the power of mythic and superstitious thinking as the thought went fleetingly through my mind that I, an agnostic, might be giving God, if he did exist, an idea I would not want him to carry out, a joke on me for inadvertently giving myself an added day of life beyond what he prescribed. That, it struck me, was the magic, based on fear, that so often underlies belief. It was also recognition that we who think God might or could exist must also acknowledge that the vagaries of life that might point to his existence reveal an anthropomorphic sense of irony and gallows humor. Such a God can listen in, hear our thoughts, and play wantonly with us if he wishes. God as ultimate cosmic joker or ironist or mind reader! It is, of course, all possible, since it cannot be disproven.

Few felt the cruelty of God the dark, cosmic joker as did Mark Twain. After going bankrupt following some bad investments, after suffering the death of his older daughter, Susy, from meningitis, after seeing another daughter, Jean, diagnosed as epileptic, and while watching his wife's and his own health decline, Twain took all this as a personal attack and railed against God. The Mark Twain who wrote *Letters from the Earth* and *The Mysterious Stranger* is a man who blasphemed God and religion and appeared to reject both out of deep personal anger. But paradoxically, he also confirmed his belief in God's existence by taking God to task for his harshness. Herman Melville, too, expressed terrible anger at God and considered *Moby-Dick*, as he described it in a letter to Hawthorne, "a wicked book." By the end of his life he was agnostic. Despite what one of his biographers, Lawrance Thompson, aptly called his quarrel with God, Melville still longed for the God he felt comforted by as a boy — before his father died a terrible death and Melville's seafaring experiences changed, for the rest of his life, his view of the Almighty. He too saw God as a cosmic joker playing mercilessly with our lives.

It occurred to me, as I thought of all the negative reactions to God by those who saw him as a cruel humorist for causing needless suffering, that negative theology might be a more fitting way to understand God — by describing not what God is but what he is not. Or to look at it another way, by recognizing that what we call God is beyond our perception, beyond existence, even beyond time and space, ineffable. Krishna's words to Arjuna in the Bhagavad Gita are instructive. When we seek the Atman or Nirvana — or some other removal from ego and from what Hindu and Buddhist belief see as the illusion of our lives — we are thwarted because we live in the mortal realm. We must realize that the mortal coil we call our lives is unreal, and is not God.

But what if — and what-ifs are often the key to imaginative and religious thinking of all varieties — what if the real cosmic joke is that the God of our fathers and mothers, the God many millions of the earth's passengers have believed in, really is that God: the God who gave us commandments to live by; the God who looks over us and constantly tests our belief in him via the free will he gave us, along with reason to doubt; and the God from whom all blessings and suffering, and the very existence of all earth's species, and good and evil, derive? What if the real litmus test for us is his being real to us, real enough to make us abandon our paltry intellect that challenges his existence, and abandon all the negativity associated with not believing in him because of the world's suffering and evil? What if, unlike Twain and Melville, we did not take personally God's action or inaction but simply believed? Or what if I rejected agnosticism and the idea of a personal code, and suddenly felt his presence capture my entire being?

No more spiritual hunger. No more spiritual envy. God now speaks directly to me, undeniably and beyond any rational explanation. I feel God, and God makes me feel wonder and awe. I know the certainty of his majesty and his love for me and my fellow creatures. I see a blinding light in a vivid dream or while awake, or I envision the path ascending to the Godhead, which at last is clear and luminous, beyond doubt. An angel appears like a theatrical deus ex machina on the proscenium of life's stage, an indisputable sign demonstrating to me God's munificence, his power, and grandeur, and I am gripped with awe and transformed in ways I never could have conceived.

Or there he is, Jesus, the son of Ha Shem, incarnate but recognizable to me as the good Lord Jesus, coming for the second time, for me to witness with my mortal sight, and he offers me, the unfit mortal, God's gift of grace, the washing away of all my sins, a cleansing in the blood of the lamb and his holy blood, the blood he sacrificed by dying on the cross for me and all of us — including, one might suppose, Hindus, Buddhists, Muslims, and all of the nonbelievers. I suddenly know beyond doubt that Christ suffered and died for me, that all my transgressions are forgiven, and that I am to be granted the keys to the gates of heaven and am given the promise of life eternal. I know that Jesus loves me unconditionally, that I am forgiven for all trespasses, and I embrace the trinity of God the father, his only son, and the Holy Ghost, and abjure the unholy agnostic trinity of Robert Ingersoll, T. H. Huxley, and Bertrand Russell. To any who will listen, I passionately tell my story of having been lost but then found, cradled, and comforted at last in the redemptive and all-embracing divine love of Christ, the savior, my savior.

Or yet another scenario to sate my spiritual hunger and vanquish spiritual envy: the separation between me and the world outside me no longer appears real, and I am one with spirit beyond matter, one with all my fellow creatures and with nature, ecstatic in my new, higher sphere of being, able to see at last what before was unseeable. I experience a spiritual awakening that opens my eyes to what lies beyond the veiled world I thought I was in, to a new, multichromatic vision, where I see everything through new eyes and feel the ecstasy of higher consciousness and become an avatar of heretofore unoccupied being.

These are stories for revival meetings or rapt New Age audiences or spiritual seekers. They are stories that those who believe or want to believe love to hear and feel inspired by. If any such stories were mine to tell, I would tell them with drama and flair, and hope I could find a good agent. With an oratorical gift and panache, the kind that can sway large numbers, who knows what kind of attention or purse-filling results I might garner. I am not trying to sound cynical. I am trying to say there are greater personal rewards, and often larger worldly rewards, for the believer who, like Saint Paul at Damascus, has a gripping story to tell that involves finding faith or belief or God or transformation of the spirit in the midst of a spiritual desert of nonbelief. Agnosticism is obviously not compelling to the believer or the spiritual seeker. How much more appealing to those comforted by religious or spiritual belief, those who fervently seek answers, is the odyssey that starts with doubt and disbelief and ends with the wonders of spiritual reward, with an experience of God or Jesus or at-oneness with the cosmos. Feelings of awe, wonder, and spiritual elevation sure beat the hell out of dull, everyday transience.

Chaucer's Pardoner is an archetypal example of the man who would use belief for personal profit and prey on true believers by selling bogus relics, such as splinters of the cross or Saint John the Baptist's jawbone, or cures or indulgences that purchasers believe will free them from their sins. Or think of those two ultimately tarred-and-feathered con men of Mark Twain's, the Duke and the Dauphin in *Huckleberry Finn*. The hypocrites who swindle believers out of their hard-earned money are morally opprobrious to most ethical agnostics and atheists, as well as to believers. American civilization has seen a host of religious confidence men and charlatans, its Elmer Gantrys of every religious and spiritual stripe, its religious Bernard Madoffs. Then there are those who are mad, insane with religious fervor and zealotry. The Reverend Jim Jones, who literally seduced and fleeced his flock, is an extreme example of the type of person who misuses religion to take advantage of the reverence and goodness of. well-meaning believers. A paranoid lunatic, he bilked them and then took them off to Guyana, where most of them died in a combination mass suicide and mass murder when they drank, or were forced to drink, poison.

Of course there are sincere and altruistic men and women of religious faith who have led their flocks with higher moral purpose and a keen and abiding faith. How could there not be? But is it possible that our earthly existence was set in motion by a divine planner without a plan, a cosmic joker-playwright who put us on the stage of life, as Beckett did Estragon and Vladimir, just to see where our trust and belief and faith would lead us over ages of accursed time? Beckett, who claimed to remember being in the womb, called *Waiting for Godot* a tragicomedy, not a cometragedy. Which of those two best describes your life?

Now that I've become a bona fide elder, I am waiting for the ultimate cosmic joke — death. Unless we cotton to poet Robert Lowell, who advises "Cut your own throat. Now! Now!" or we in some other fashion cut short our life spans, we all wait. We are sentenced to capital punishment for the crime of a birth we had no complicity in. We remain awake for a brief time and then sleep and rot, our bones decaying, each of our bodies a memento mori for those who live on. As Peggy Lee sang, "Is that all there is?" Can that be it? My parents both began the descent into death's clutches frightened and helpless, and then developed dementia, even their memories of passion, love, joy, and tenderness obliterated. After all the anxiety and Sturm und Drang of life, that was how it ended. To think of lives that meant so much coming to so little — was it a cosmic joke?

Though I remain agnostic, I nevertheless believe this one life is all there is. And as I get older, I find myself musing, as I did when I was a boy, about my funeral. Huck Finn got the gift of seeing his, but most of us can only imagine what our funerals might be like or who will attend. I was reminded that I'm getting nearer to the end by unsolicited information I received in the mail from the Trident Society informing me that I could avoid a funeral altogether and prepare for my own cremation. How will I be remembered and mourned? What kind of legacy, if any, will I leave my children and posterity? These are hardly idle questions we ask ourselves, but they are self-indulgent. There is narcissistic pleasure in thinking of oneself as appreciated and beloved and missed, and as having possibly created something meaningful to pass on. When I think of facing death as I age, I think mostly of my parents and their slow wasting away, but I also think of two of my friends.

Irv was a friend and colleague who was also a holocaust literature scholar. Some of us who were his friends would joke about how much he suffered in life. It was not only that he stared into the flames of the holocaust as a scholar and became obsessed by the suffering of those who had experienced it, but also that he carried suffering around with him as if it were an old, odd-fitting coat. Irv seemed as if he were made to suffer. The word that best fit him was *lugubrious*. I used to say that he was the kind of man who could spend the rest of eternity pouring over the records and videos at Yad Vashem, Israel's memorial to the holocaust.

Dr. Tamkin says in *Seize the Day*, a novel by Saul Bellow, a writer Irv loved, that "some people are married to suffering," and "if they go with joy they think it's adultery." Tamkin's words fit Irv. Yet I also have a different sort of image from right before his death that stays with me. He is lying in his hospital deathbed, knowing full well that the cancer is eating him away and only days remain. His three children are at his bedside. He is laughing. His face is suffused with joy. I had never seen him happier or more glowing or more at peace. All the yapping we hear — the choruses of rhetoric about dying a good death, and death with dignity, and the courage necessary to face death and resign oneself to it, and live in the here and now — and here was Irv, ready to exit with joy on his face and love and laughter in his heart! What a cosmic joke that a man who suffered throughout his life could find at the very end a joy he never imagined. Or perhaps the cosmic joke was that he never suffered better than at the end.

What we talk about when we talk about death is often its mystery and its certainty, and the talk, it seems, is an unconscious attempt to dispel or exorcise both, or to dissemble or defend against them. A cardiologist friend and I were talking about death. He had recently converted to atheism after reading Richard Dawkins. My friend had saved many lives and had many times seen "that bloody motor," as Grace Paley called the heart, simply cease. He understood, better than most, how narrow the threads of life can be. "I know," he said to me with the kind of confidence that has helped make him a trusted and gifted physician and a good and loving husband, father, and grandfather, "that were I to die today, it would be okay. I would be fine with it. I've lived nearly seventy years and had a full and fulfilling life and done most everything I set out to do. I could die without regret." Does it, I wonder, get any better than that? Can one ask for more from topsy-turvy life, which can seem like a cosmic joke, doomed to conclude yet yield no answers?

Chapter 16

SEPARATING THE AGNOSTICS FROM THE HERDS

et's get to the pith. Agnostics have nothing to die for except the death that ends our lives. I've often asked myself: What would I die for? What is worth giving up one's life for, especially if there is likely no life after? If not for belief, or for one's loved ones, then the options dwindle. This vale of tears could be the preparation for a future spent among seraphim and harps, or in a burning inferno of hot coals and pitchforks. But if there is a wager to be made, I would bet against either. Camus tells us in *The Myth of Sisyphus* that the only real philosophical question is whether to commit suicide. But a larger question, it seems to me, is the question of what, if anything, is worth dying for?

The elevations of joy, the precious moments worth savoring, in my adult agnostic life have been ephemeral, and even the most blissful ephemeral moments do not seem to lend themselves to the ultimate sacrifice. One usually needs to believe in the absolute to be willing to give up one's life. I love

my country and feel patriotic, but would I die for my country?
Would I have given up my life in the just war against Hitler? I
believe so, but as in the case of belief in God, I'd need to know,
were I to cede my life, the what and the why. Whether one
will give up life for any cause or purpose or blissful moment
can be impossible to predict. Yet I have said that I respect the
rights of those who choose to believe, or not to believe, so long
as they do no harm. But what about those who choose to harm
themselves by dying for a cause or choosing self-martyrdom?
Should any of that matter to me?

I have been emphasizing a code of respect for others and
for what they believe or do not believe. It boils down to recognizing that what people believe, or how they worship or act
or don't act on their belief or nonbelief, is, as my Dad would
have jauntily put it, their own damn business as long as they
do no harm.

When I was in Texas doing a job for Electronic Data Systems, a company once controlled by Ross Perot, my father
was dying, and some of the EDS people I worked with who
knew this told me with decency and kindness that they would
pray for him. One older woman named Doris asked me my
father's name and told me she would ask her minister, a man
she assured me was "close to the Lord," to pray for my father by name. I thought it funny that this Christian man of
the cloth in the Lone Star State would be sending up a prayer
to Jesus for a Jewish stranger named Hyman in the Buckeye
State. But I was touched by the faith and kindness shown me
by this woman and the others who said they would pray for
my dad, touched by their earnest concern and their unasked-
for offer to pray for the health of a man they would never
meet. I thought, at the time, who knows what good it might
actually do?

I could as easily have been contemptuous, or felt certain the prayers would be useless, and branded these well-meaning folks, as some atheists might have, Texas fools, but I felt touched and thought there was no harm in their praying — though I could imagine a hardened atheist saying defiantly, "I don't want your useless prayers to a God who does not exist." It seems to me that many atheists are like that, like fundamentalists in their intolerance and as obdurate in their opposition to faith as the fundamentalists can be in belief. Someone pious like Doris ought to realize, however, and graciously accept, the fact that an atheist can be as certain there is no God who hears prayer, as she is that there is one who does. Tolerance and understanding are, ideally, two-way streets. Problems occur when each side demands these streets be one-way, their way, and brings up matters of public policy, like a national day of prayer, or prayer in school, or God help us (as my mother would have prefaced it), abortion.

I have been criticized for being too respectful of the pro-life crusaders I have had on my radio program. I am on the side of those who call themselves pro-choice, but I respect the fact that those opposed to abortion may be motivated not by attempts to keep women from making choices on their own but by their belief that life begins at conception. There are, of course, atheists and agnostics opposed to abortion. But society cannot abide the lawbreaker who — like the killer of the abortion doctor George Tiller, who clearly believed he was saving the lives of infant humans — decides to play God and kill an abortionist or bomb an abortion clinic.

I was struck by Doris's faith that her minister had prayer power, faith that he was, as she put it, close to the Lord, and touched that she was concerned enough about me to ask such a person to pray for my dying father. Of course, I did not believe prayers would wrest my father from the jaws of death, yet because of the kindness and sincerity of people like Doris, I find it an important part of my personal code to respect belief simply because I realize it can be tied to decency and compassion, which warrants the same in return.

I wondered, too, about Doris's close-to-the-Lord minister. Was he another charlatan, or was he sincere? I admit that I am skeptical of men or women of the cloth who believe they have a special channel of communication. Some prey on, more than pray for, their parishioners. Or they line their pockets, or are bedeviled by compulsions that seem to fuel their belief, or that are fueled by their belief, compulsions like the lustful demons of pederastic priests, or of the Reverend Jimmy Swaggart, who could not stay away from prostitutes, or of the Reverend Jim Bakker, who could not stay away from Jessica Hahn, or of the rabbi who specialized in working with youth who was caught by an NBC sting operation set up to ensnare pedophiles. Intense belief can coexist with, and combine with, lust, narcissism, sexual perversion, or avarice or other forms or covetousness and produce a potent brew. Atheists and agnostics are hardly immune to any of these; unless they endeavor to live by a moral or ethical code, they can end up as hypocritical as those who believe in religious morality but fail to practice it.

Jim Jones urged charity and good works, perhaps for the same reasons Mao and Castro did, but perhaps also out of a sense of duty to God and the religious beliefs he would dishonor. But think of the agnostic. What does he or she have to gain by saying I don't know? Can someone be a charlatan or a manipulator of souls or an egregious hypocrite when one admits that he or she has no answers and cannot offer a path to truth or light or certainty other than a morphing code he or she may be earnestly trying to live by? If one manages to bring in followers through the power of the certainty, or the uncertainty of uncertainty, or has the charisma to be — like many men of God and a fair number of women of God — a pied piper of agnostic belief, where can one's followers be led? How would one enrich one's pockets by attempting to proselytize with discourses in agnosticism?

Many atheists of the present atheist zeitgeist — Harris, Dawkins, Hitchens, Dennett, and Jacoby — attract followers largely because they, too, offer certainty, the surety that belief in God and faith are toxic and scornworthy. Does this mean agnostics, who cannot offer certainty, are morally superior to atheists? Hardly. But I am talking about agnosticism, not secularism. When the British novelist Martin Amis, another diehard atheist, suggested that secularists don't shout "Allah Akbar" and kill people, the literary critic and former Stanford professor Marjorie Perloff responded by saying that they shout, "Heil Hitler." A secularist can still believe in a political ideology like Nazism or Communism, but a full agnostic, the kind I am, is in a state of waiting that obviates belief. I favor using *agnosticism* to signify nonacceptance of all forms of dogmatic certainty — religious as well as ideological — in the absence of empirical proof.

Is it not a better option to trust agnosticism, even if it seems wishy-washy, since it is difficult to use the absence of belief, or the certainty or uncertainty of uncertainty, for coercive or venal purposes (though there are doubtless agnostics of low and venal character)? There are also likely agnostics who enjoy undermining or tricking the religious or the devout. But the reason many individuals have a brief against religion, belief, ideology, or dogma is that they see not only uncertainty but also the destructive consequences of certainty.

Yet, like me, they can nevertheless respect well-intentioned and generous forms of certainty. The doubt and skepticism, or the certainty or uncertainty of uncertainty recognized by agnostics, in contrast to the certainty of atheists and believers, seem hardly likely to lead to either proselytizing or coercion.

When I was in graduate school, there was a silly cheer that beer drinkers liked to sing that went: My name is Jesus the son of God. Hello hello hello hello hello. I come to save you and heal your bod. Hello hello hello hello. Rock 'em. Sock 'em. Yaaaaay, God! The parodic rah-rah quality of the song scarcely conceals the implicit powers Jesus was believed to possess that are reflected in the lyrics. Cheerleading is more a hallmark of religious believers and atheists than of agnostics. Years after I became a professor, a graduate student of mine, a sweet young Christian woman whose parents were missionaries, told me that her husband had gone through the intellectual torment of losing his faith in Christ. He had studied other religious beliefs and the writings of religious doubters and naysayers, but eventually had come back to the sanctity of even-firmer belief in Christianity, realizing that the doubt he had gone through was good for him, since it made his Christian belief stronger. No more would he stray to the ideas that took Jesus off the cross and into the realm of skepticism or doubt.

My student told this story to me with eyes shining and brimming. She wasn't proselytizing. She was radiating happiness at a story that reinforced the faith she and her husband shared. I imagined how fellow believers must have felt hearing the story she told, and how it probably stirred them and touched their hearts. I would venture that even a great orator like Ingersoll couldn't stir others quite like that. There is no rah-rah power in agnosticism. It enters through the intellect, not through the emotions. Stories or chants or affirmations of belief have emotional effects. Stories of uncertainty usually do not. And if tolerance is a virtue, one must concede that uncertainty, by its nature, is probably more conducive to it.

I add a couple of stories of my own here. I was once moved to tears by a young woman singing "Ave Maria." She was fifteen years old and had what is often described as the voice of an angel. It is easy to see how someone with strong religious belief would think such a voice a gift from God, especially when listening to a religious song like "Ave Maria," a beautiful melodic prayer to the holy mother of Christ. I was moved emotionally despite having no personal religious belief. Religious belief is exploitable, but so is belief in nothing. I know it is easy for nonbelievers who disdain religion to feel contempt for strong and ardent believers. Much of that contempt was exacerbated in the United States with the rise of evangelical political power during the George W. Bush administration and the murders by Islamic fanatics on 9-11.

Many nonbelievers view those who have religious zeal as evil or simpleminded, and many nonbelievers see the zealous, especially the most fanatical, as hypocritical, even truly baleful. Much as I respect Hitchens and Dawkins, I sensed, when I interviewed them, their intellectual arrogance toward those who were, from their point of view, naive and foolish enough to embrace organized religion or other religious belief systems. But I have known many bright, generous true believers. If they can secure inner peace or turn what may be their darker impulses into action of a higher order, then let them wear their religion on both sleeves, so long as they do not foist it on others.

I recall driving back to Ohio from Madison, Wisconsin, when I was a graduate student and hitting a snowstorm in

Indiana that paralyzed my old and terribly infirm Pontiac. Some local Hoosiers saw my distress and came to my aid, insisting on digging me out of the snow with their shovels and towing me to a nearby gas station, where a friend of theirs, a mechanic, repaired my car. I wanted to pay them, but they firmly refused to take my money — which admittedly wasn't much. They spoke of wanting to be good Samaritans and then chatted with me about their activity in a church study group that stressed performing Good Samaritan acts.

They also spoke of their support for the war in Vietnam, which I was adamantly opposed to, and when I heard their views on the war, I found myself wondering, having heard many stories about how pervasive the Klan once was in Indiana, whether they might be unsheeted Klan members. I spoke guardedly about my opposition to the war, but our discussion was an amiable exchange of opinions. Had they been actual Klansmen, I would have had serious moral qualms about their good deeds on my behalf, but their position on the war, though muddleheaded and morally wrong from my point of view, struck me as sincere and motivated by patriotism and fear of godless communism. They seemed to be people at peace with themselves. How could I be contemptuous of that?

I envied what I recognized as the comfort and certainty and peace that belief can engender. I contrast the experience I had with those Hoosiers to an experience a fellow grad student and poet-friend had in Madison with a religious God-Firster who was also a strong supporter of the Vietnam War. In a bar outside of town, David, the poet, and this fellow got into a heated discussion about the war. The guy kept telling David that he needed to understand the real reason for the Indochina war, which, the fellow insisted, was the necessity to slice off the tentacles of a godless ideology that would shut down churches and impose both totalitarianism and tyrannically run collective farms, crushing the rights Americans had known since the revolution against England and making atheism the law of our land. David argued with the guy, and both became more lubricated with booze, until the guy, mouthing clichés about honest differences of opinion that good Christians could overcome, extended his hand in peace and offered to drive David, who was without transportation, to his apartment. When they got to David's place, the guy opened his glove compartment, took out a Saturday night special, shot David in both of his legs, and then opened the car door and shoved him out.

In relating these stories from my days as a graduate student in Wisconsin, I have inadvertently stepped into a parable about two sides of human character. Both sides can, like selfishness and altruism, be contained in the same human. I don't understand why, to quote Raymond Carver, we do the things we do. Why is one person a Samaritan and another a trigger puller? The trigger puller might have told himself he was obeying the sixth commandment not to kill, since he shot David in his legs rather than in the chest or head. And perhaps the Indiana Samaritans who helped me out gratis with my car were also thieves or adulterers or even murderers. We operate by our own moral navigation system whether we like to believe we do or not. We form our codes of ethics apart from God because the authentic authorship of God's words, either on tablets or in scripture, cannot be known, and even if it could be, people could still operate in whatever ways they choose.

As an agnostic, I have felt compelled to work out my own personal code, but in the final analysis, where morality is concerned I am who I am, tied to my own time and place. Would

I be as concerned with the welfare of others, or consider the importance of others in a personal code, if I were driven solely by survival? The continuum of good and evil behavior is vast and our species capable of an incredible variety of acts, whereas moral accountings change, and often change radically, with systems of belief and place and time.

Chapter 17

PEACE UNTO THEE AND ME, AND
AN OLD ELVIS TOP-TEN HIT

hy seek to find, let alone hope to find answers to, what appears unknowable? One might just as well ask why seek knowledge. Curiosity and inquisitiveness prompt us to search, and both intense desire for knowledge and spiritual hunger can drive volition. We search for truth or meaning even if the quest brings neither. But there is another reason why the spiritual life, or the lives of the God-finders in the thrall of his love, stirs envy in this agnostic's breast. In many instances, it is people who cleave to faith and belief who seem much more apt to find what for many of us is elusive — inner peace. I for one would welcome it. Poll after poll and empirical research reveal that people with rock-solid faith, who are not fanatical about it, are happier, more content, more at peace. I don't mean they experience only transitory inner peace. I mean something closer to serenity, an abiding peace that seems to come from emotion-based belief.

An agnostic sociologist I had occasion to interview, Phil Zuckerman, wrote the book *Society without God* about the

Danes and how content they seem — Denmark scores high on the so-called happiness index and low on violent crime and corruption — despite low church attendance and a general lack of God in their daily lives. The book is based on a lot of anecdotal evidence, and Zuckerman acknowledges that many Danes still have baptisms and church weddings, but, he argues, Denmark is a nation mostly removed from God and yet generally at peace. Of course, as I pointed out during our conversation on the air, Denmark is a pretty homogenous society with state support for its citizens from womb to tomb. But I concede Zuckerman's point that Danes appear to be more at peace (he also mentions the notoriously melancholy Swedes), though I still favor the argument that those of greater faith are more likely to find inner peace.

Some of my inability to achieve inner peace no doubt has to do with temperament, drive, set points, personality, neurosis, or perhaps even my DNA. But I know there are other agnostics who, like me, have tried to find or follow their bliss, to use Joseph Campbell's phrase, and have been unsuccessful. Bliss, never easy to define, fortunately has many sources, though for nonbelievers it is transitory and temporal and not necessarily allied with inner peace. Bliss can come, often accompanied by inner peace, from spiritual sustenance or belief in God and the eternal.

Elvis Presley, no stranger to gospel or religious hymns, had a major hit song in 1965 called "Crying in the Chapel," which begins:

> You saw me crying in the chapel.
> The tears I shed were tears of joy.
> I know the meaning of contentment now.
> I am happy with the Lord.

There it is. Joy and contentment and happiness from belief all expressed in the chapel, a good, ecumenical, interfaith
name for a house of worship, the dwelling place of God, the
place where one can be close to him and feel his presence and
feel enveloped by his love. Who wouldn't envy such peace?
T. S. Eliot concludes *The Waste Land* with the poetic utterance, three times, of the Sanskrit word *Shantih*, which translates to "the peace which passeth understanding." Is such
peace even possible for the restless and neuroticized human
spirit, or for the inquisitive agnostic who cannot fathom or
find belief? What of those agnostics who meditate? The other
Sanskrit words in *The Waste Land*, which are from the Upanishads, are *Datta*, *Dayadhavam*, and *Damyata*, most often
translated as the human requirement to give, to sympathize,
and to control. Are these ingredients for a peace that extends
beyond understanding? There is, of course, no formula for
inner peace, any more than there is for world peace. (I'm afraid
all that creative visualization urged on by bumper stickers
didn't cinch it.) But those of great faith and spiritual practice
can, it seems, attain it or get near it. If religion can be the ve-
hicle to inner peace, why knock it?

Jesus was known as the prince of peace, and his good office was to bring everlasting peace and transformation of the
creature self, the individual born in sin unable to fend off de-
sires. We see hope for peace reflected in the common saluta-
tion of Muslims and Jews: "Assalaam Alaykum" or "Shalom
Aleikkem," or "Peace be unto you." This is not so much the
Christian hope of peace tied to the spirit of Christmas —
peace on earth — but more the hope for a personal peace, one
that can come to an individual from God. Words from the
book Numbers, in the Old Testament, that are often included
at the end of rabbinical blessings during Jewish services are a

request for God to grant personal peace: "May the Lord lift
his countenance upon you and give you peace." We are not
speaking here of white doves and of nation not lifting sword
up against nation. We are speaking of the internal peace that
Eliot's Fisher King in *The Waste Land* could find by "shor-
ing up his fragments" — that is, the sum of his experiences,
the rituals and myths and motifs of the poem — and listening
to what the thunder said and obeying the commands of the
Upanishads. It is a peace promised to the person of faith, to
the spiritual seeker able to trod the sanctified and blessed path.

Strong faith and religious belief can bring solace, comfort, hope, regeneration, and ultimately peace to — let us call
them — those blessed individuals who feel that God or the
spirit of the universe will deliver them from creature evils and
reward them with what they believe they most profoundly
need. For an agnostic to find a personal code that establishes
the boundaries of good and evil without the Ten Commandments or some other God-made laws is a challenge that seems
frankly less formidable than finding personal peace. The full
acceptance of ignorance and the inability to fill the heart with
faith or belief can truly seem like temporal limbo — as often
happens with hearts that are restless, wild, and full of inconsistencies and antipodes. Faith and the peace it can bring — let
us be realistic — can of course also be the result of simple-
mindedness or rank stupidity. But unvarnished, resolute faith
can hasten inner peace.

Chapter 18

SOME FINAL THOUGHTS

$\mathcal{A}$rthur Eddington, the British astronomer who gave us (and novelist Martin Amis) the concept of time as an arrow, also posited that randomness could not be undone in a physical world governed by entropy and the second law of thermodynamics, which states that a closed system of energy cannot have what it started with, and usable energy is lost in the form of unusable energy. In other words, change over time also means decline, dissipation of energy, and an inevitable loss of molecular force. Thomas Pynchon brought James Maxwell's "demon" to popular attention in his novel *The Crying of Lot 49*, the intellectually tantalizing idea that the second law of thermodynamics can be violated. Physical laws of the universe are subject to change, and indeed our understanding of them has changed over the course of time, but via research, study, and the compilation of empirical observations, we can chart many of the laws and understand their trajectories. Religious and spiritual laws also change with fluctuations and illuminations in science and belief. Cultural views and historic shifts doubtless will continue to change our attitudes, including attitudes toward God and the Ten Commandments.

When I began writing, I was looking for an equation that might give moral credence to the Ten Commandments and explain why they ought to be believed, beyond the reason that God gave them to Moses, and even beyond traditional legal or secular institutionalized rationales. I wanted to see if I could make sense out of my personal lifetime of questioning. I didn't know what I believed. Writing this book has not illuminated most of the dark metaphysical or moral corners that I had hoped might be illuminated. But I do believe in the power of asking the right, or most reasonable and compelling, questions, and I believe in making you, the reader, think.

I don't think I have found answers here. I have not come closer to understanding why I should accept or reject the notion of a God beyond what I am capable of fathoming. I still want to know how I, or any agnostic, can feed what may well be innate spiritual hunger when faced with an unremitting vision of spiritual and metaphysical uncertainty and a life fated to expire and a species and a planet all quite possibly moving toward extinction. I want, too, as a self-identifying Jew, and in the face of my agnosticism, to discover how to maintain the precious Jewish identity handed down to me historically and genetically, to identify as a Jew even though the Jewish religion is rooted in monotheism and the inimitable power of the one living omnipotent God.

I was once approached on the campus where I currently teach by a member of the group Jews for Jesus. He wanted to tell me the good news that he had found Jesus Christ, and I, younger and more foolish, went into a serious explanation of how you cannot be a Jew and be for Jesus. Those who claimed to be both Jews and believers in Jesus, I argued, were simply those who wanted it both ways, wanted to keep their heritage but also to gain acceptance from Christians who believed the messianic prophecy of the Old Testament had been brought to fruition with the virgin birth. After establishing what I felt was a convincing argument, I paused, and the young man, who had seemed to be giving me and my reasoned discourse his full attention, simply shouted with a gust of sudden emotion, "Praise Jesus!"

My code of tolerance for the beliefs of others insists on allowing for what others believe so long as they do not try to force it on other people or do harm in its name. This exposition has been less a brief for agnosticism than my spelling out why agnosticism, above all other beliefs or nonbeliefs, makes the greatest amount of reasoned sense — which, I suppose, makes it indeed a brief and perhaps even a polemic for agnosticism, if only by default. Atheism, or the absence of God, cannot be proven any more than religious faith can be.

I had a curious onstage conversation about Judaism and Buddhism a number of years ago in an Oakland synagogue with the late Alan Lew, a conservative rabbi schooled in Buddhist meditation. We spoke of the phenomenon of what some call Jew-Boos or Bagel Buddhists, of whom there are many in the San Francisco Bay Area, born-and-raised Jews who have turned to Buddhism. How, I asked, could Judaism and Buddhism be hybridized when the role God plays in one is irreconcilable with the role he plays in the other? But if Buddhist meditation brings intimations of greater peace, who should care if Judaism is diluted? A reform rabbi in Marin County — where I have made my home for four decades — announced from the pulpit a number of years ago that he was an agnostic. Some congregants were upset, but the majority weren't. Why should they be? It was Freud who said that Moses could be removed from the Jewish religion and, unlike Christianity if Christ were removed, the Jewish religion would still exist without Moses — though not without God. The teachings of the Buddha — the tools of mindfulness, lovingkindness, and compassion — can certainly exist independently of the Buddha. But what is Judaism, a God-centered religion, without God or with the agnostic's doubt and uncertainty? Does it matter? Should it matter?

In the Jewish religion, there is a religious practice of memorializing one's loved ones on the anniversaries — in the Jewish calendar — of their deaths by lighting what is called a *yahrzeit* candle. I realized in 2009, courtesy of the Jewish funeral home in Cleveland that sends me notices with reminders of *yahrzeit* dates, that the memorial dates for both my father and my mother were on the same day in 2010. I wanted to honor their memory not because of the commandment that bid me to honor them, or because, as both my mother and father believed, God was watching over us all and was involved in our lives. I wanted to honor their memory simply to do so and to maintain a tradition, a ritual, that I had been introduced to when I was a boy as I watched my parents light *yahrzeit* candles for their parents.

Consider if you will one final song lyric, the opening of a folk song about Moses sung by the folk trio Peter, Paul, and Mary:

> There was a man come into Egypt, and Moses was his name
> When he saw the grief upon us,
> In his heart there burned a flame.

Flames burn until they are extinguished. The flame of liberty that Moses brought when the Jews were emancipated from

Egyptian bondage is the theme of the song, and this flame is worth keeping bright by humankind, which is worthy, we can only hope, of the many lives sacrificed. Agnostics can be selective about keeping the Ten Commandments or believing they were handed to Moses at Sinai by God or by another. Lighting candles in memory of one's parents, barring a possible accidental fire breaking out, can't hurt. Neither can saying Kaddish, the ritual prayer for the dead that is in reality a sanctification of God. God, after all, might be somewhere watching, for all we know, seeing the candle's flame, hearing the mourner's prayer.

Acknowledgments

$\mathcal{J}$ would like to extend my thanks to those who were kind enough to provide useful answers to the questions I asked: Robert Alter, George Lakoff, Jacob Needleman, and Marilyn Yalom. I also would like to extend thanks to Louise Kollenbaum, Mary Lamia, Les Marks, Gerald Nachman, Robyn Russell, Eric Solomon, Susan Wels, and Manfred Wolf. Special thanks to Marc Allen, Georgia Hughes, Kristen Cashman, Jonathan Wichmann, Monique Muhlenkamp, and the rest of the devoted crew at New World Library; to Bonnie Hurd for her smart copyediting; to my agent, Amy Rennert; and to my not-so-secret editorial weapons — Lauren and Alexa and (especially) Leslie Krasny.

Index

A

abolitionist movement, 155

abortion, 219

Abraham, 71, 73

action, 83–84

acts of God, 204–5

Adonai, 72, 73–74

adultery, commandment against, 35–39

Afghanistan War (2001–), 139

After Auschwitz (Rubenstein), 19

afterlife, 31–32, 98–99, 202, 217

aggression, evil as, 185

agnosticism/agnostics

    AA chapters, 101

    as altruists, 201–6

    archetypal premise of, 90–92

    atheism contrasted with, 6–7, 94, 109–10

    author as, 25–27, 99, 101–2, 103, 149, 152, 182–83, 185–86

    benefits of rejecting, 209–11

    change and, 96–97

    coincidences and, 117, 120, 123

    death and, 217–18

    etymology of, 8, 94

    evil and, 182–83, 185–86

    as floating signifier, 93, 95

    God's existence and, 86

    humor about, 65

    inner peace and, 228, 230

    morality and, 2, 31–33, 46–49, 65–69

    notable figures in, 94–95, 97–98

    origins of, 103

    paranormal and, 127–28

    Pascal's wager and, 98–99

    as personal, 103–5

    polemical writing on, 8

    prayer and, 25–26, 99, 101

    questioning as heart of, 6, 81

    religion as viewed by, 158–59

    skeptic tradition in, 138

    soulful experience and, 199–200

    spiritual envy and, 141, 145, 146

    Ten Commandments and, 25–27

    about time, 163–64

    true believer reaction to, 110–11

    uncertainty and, 6, 94, 102, 110, 114, 151, 221–23

    varied meanings of, 93–94, 102–3

    See also Huxley, Thomas H.; Ingersoll, Robert G.; Russell, Bertrand

Agnosticism (Flint), 103

Agnostic's Apology, An (Stephens), 102

AIDS, 203

alcohol, 172

Alcoholics Anonymous, 100–101, 158

alien abductions, research on, 135–37

Allah, 73–74, 143

Allende, Isabel, 115, 116

Alter, Robert, 72

altruism. *See* good deeds, doing

American Atheists, 152–53

American Buddhists, 144

American culture. *See* United States

"Am I an Atheist or an Agnostic?" (Russell), 109–10

Amis, Martin, 221, 231

Andy S. (author's neighbor), 51–53

Anna Karenina (Tolstoy), 36

anthropomorphic taboos, 73

approval of others, seeking, 190–91

Arendt, Hannah, 186

Aristotle, 20, 57

Armenians, Turkish violence against, 186

Armstrong, Karen, 35

Arnold, Matthew, 57–58

art, 67, 200–201

Art S. (greaser), 184–85

asceticism, 134

Asherah (Semitic deity), 82

astrology, 159

$\mathcal{M}$ ichael Krasny, PhD, hosts the nation's most listened-to locally produced public radio talk show, *Forum with Michael Krasny*. A widely published scholar and literary critic, he is an English professor at San Francisco State University and has taught at Stanford University and University of California, San Francisco. *Forum* is heard weekdays on KQED-FM in San Francisco, an affiliate of National Public Radio, as well as on Sirius-XM satellite radio. The many awards he has received include the S. Y. Agnon Gold Medal for Intellectual Distinction, the Eugene Block Award for Human Rights Journalism, the National Public Radio Award from the American Publishers Association, the Silver Medallion from the California Bar Association, and the Inclusiveness in Media Award from the National Conference for Community and Justice. His television work has been honored with two Emmy nominations. He has interviewed many of the great cultural icons of our era and is also the author of *Off Mike: A Memoir of Talk Radio and Literary Life* (Stanford University Press) and coauthor of *Sound Ideas* (McGraw-Hill). The Teaching Company has released his *Masterpieces of Short Fiction*, a series of twenty-four lectures on DVD and audio. He lives in the San Francisco Bay Area. To learn more:

www.kqed.org/radio/programs/forum/

NEW WORLD LIBRARY is dedicated to publishing books and other media that inspire and challenge us to improve the quality of our lives and the world.

We are a socially and environmentally aware company, and we strive to embody the ideals presented in our publications. We recognize that we have an ethical responsibility to our customers, our staff members, and our planet.

We serve our customers by creating the finest publications possible on personal growth, creativity, spirituality, wellness, and other areas of emerging importance. We serve New World Library employees with generous benefits, significant profit sharing, and constant encouragement to pursue their most expansive dreams.

As a member of the Green Press Initiative, we print an increasing number of books with soy-based ink on 100 percent postconsumer-waste recycled paper. Also, we power our offices with solar energy and contribute to nonprofit organizations working to make the world a better place for us all.

Our products are available
in bookstores everywhere.
For our catalog, please contact:

New World Library
14 Pamaron Way
Novato, California 94949

Phone: 415-884-2100 or 800-972-6657
Catalog requests: Ext. 50
Orders: Ext. 52
Fax: 415-884-2199
Email: escort@newworldlibrary.com

To subscribe to our electronic newsletter, visit
www.newworldlibrary.com